D0915517

Prisons

Other books in the Current Controversies series:

Prisons

James Haley, *Book Editor*

Bruce Glassman, *Vice President*
Bonnie Szumski, *Publisher*
Helen Cothran, *Managing Editor*

GREENHAVEN PRESS
An imprint of Thomson Gale, a part of The Thomson Corporation

Detroit • New York • San Francisco • San Diego • New Haven, Conn.
Waterville, Maine • London • Munich

© 2005 Thomson Gale, a part of The Thomson Corporation.

Thomson and Star Logo are trademarks and Gale and Greenhaven Press are registered trademarks used herein under license.

For more information, contact
Greenhaven Press
27500 Drake Rd.
Farmington Hills, MI 48331-3535
Or you can visit our Internet site at http://www.gale.com

LIBRARY OF CONGRESS CATALOGING-IN-PUBLICATION DATA

Prisons / James Haley, book editor.
  p. cm. — (Current controversies)
Includes bibliographical references and index.
ISBN 0-7377-2214-2 (lib. bdg. : alk. paper) —
ISBN 0-7377-2215-0 (pbk. : alk. paper)
  1. Prisons—United States. 2. Imprisonment—United States. I. Haley, James,
1968– . II. Series.
HV9471.P7822 2005
365'.973—dc22
                                                                2004047433

Printed in the United States of America

Contents

These offenders tend to behave irrationally and are thus unlikely to consider the risks of punishment.

Chapter 2: How Should Inmates Be Treated?

they pose a threat to other inmates, prison staff, and the general public. Prisons can improve the health care of inmates by providing regular screening and treatment for diseases.

Chapter 3: Should Prisons Use Inmate Labor?

Chapter 4: How Should the Prison System Be Reformed?

lower operating costs for state governments, and provide prisoners with better services than do government-run facilities.

Foreword

By definition, controversies are "discussions of questions in which opposing opinions clash" (Webster's Twentieth Century Dictionary Unabridged). Few would deny that controversies are a pervasive part of the human condition and exist on virtually every level of human enterprise. Controversies transpire between individuals and among groups, within nations and between nations. Controversies supply the grist necessary for progress by providing challenges and challengers to the status quo. They also create atmospheres where strife and warfare can flourish. A world without controversies would be a peaceful world; but it also would be, by and large, static and prosaic.

The Series' Purpose

The purpose of the Current Controversies series is to explore many of the social, political, and economic controversies dominating the national and international scenes today. Titles selected for inclusion in the series are highly focused and specific. For example, from the larger category of criminal justice, Current Controversies deals with specific topics such as police brutality, gun control, white collar crime, and others. The debates in Current Controversies also are presented in a useful, timeless fashion. Articles and book excerpts included in each title are selected if they contribute valuable, long-range ideas to the overall debate. And wherever possible, current information is enhanced with historical documents and other relevant materials. Thus, while individual titles are current in focus, every effort is made to ensure that they will not become quickly outdated. Books in the Current Controversies series will remain important resources for librarians, teachers, and students for many years.

In addition to keeping the titles focused and specific, great care is taken in the editorial format of each book in the series. Book introductions and chapter prefaces are offered to provide background material for readers. Chapters are organized around several key questions that are answered with diverse opinions representing all points on the political spectrum. Materials in each chapter include opinions in which authors clearly disagree as well as alternative opinions in which authors may agree on a broader issue but disagree on the possible solutions. In this way, the content of each volume in Current Controversies mirrors the mosaic of opinions encountered in society. Readers will quickly realize that there are many viable answers to these complex issues. By questioning each author's conclusions, students and casual readers can begin to develop the critical thinking skills so important to evaluating opinionated material.

Current Controversies is also ideal for controlled research. Each anthology in the series is composed of primary sources taken from a wide gamut of informational categories including periodicals, newspapers, books, United States and foreign government documents, and the publications of private and public organizations. Readers will find factual support for reports, debates, and research papers covering all areas of important issues. In addition, an annotated table of contents, an index, a book and periodical bibliography, and a list of organizations to contact are included in each book to expedite further research.

Perhaps more than ever before in history, people are confronted with diverse and contradictory information. During the Persian Gulf War, for example, the public was not only treated to minute-to-minute coverage of the war, it was also inundated with critiques of the coverage and countless analyses of the factors motivating U.S. involvement. Being able to sort through the plethora of opinions accompanying today's major issues, and to draw one's own conclusions, can be a complicated and frustrating struggle. It is the editors' hope that Current Controversies will help readers with this struggle.

Greenhaven Press anthologies primarily consist of previously published material taken from a variety of sources, including periodicals, books, scholarly journals, newspapers, government documents, and position papers from private and public organizations. These original sources are often edited for length and to ensure their accessibility for a young adult audience. The anthology editors also change the original titles of these works in order to clearly present the main thesis of each viewpoint and to explicitly indicate the opinion presented in the viewpoint. These alterations are made in consideration of both the reading and comprehension levels of a young adult audience. Every effort is made to ensure that Greenhaven Press accurately reflects the original intent of the authors included in this anthology.

> *"According to the Bureau of Justice Statistics, two-thirds of ex-cons are rearrested and nearly one-half are reincarcerated within three years of being released from prison."*

Introduction

In February 2001 Jean Sanders was one of the nearly six hundred thousand Americans who are released from prison each year. After release, Sanders struggled in his native Brooklyn, New York, to find a job, an apartment, and reconnect with his family, commenting, "I want a life. I want to be normal again. I want to go to work, come home, see my kids, go on vacation."

Since the mid-1970s, the United States has turned to increased incarceration to fight crime—more than 2 million Americans are now behind bars in state and federal prisons and jails. Now, thousands of ex-cons like Sanders are in the process of returning to society, and the high rate of recidivism indicates that many offenders are failing to stay out of trouble. According to the Bureau of Justice Statistics, two-thirds of ex-cons are rearrested and nearly one-half are reincarcerated within three years of being released from prison. Critics contend that prisons have become a revolving door for too many offenders. Asserts Alan Elsner, the author of *Gates of Injustice: America's Prison Crisis*, "Once they are entangled in the prison system, many [offenders] belong to it for life." Understanding the obstacles that offenders face in reentering society may provide solutions to reducing offender recidivism, and ultimately, the need to imprison so many Americans.

The use of incarceration as a crime-fighting tool accelerated in response to public concern over rising crime rates and widespread dissatisfaction with the rehabilitation and parole policies of the 1960s. Inmates who demonstrated "good behavior" or a willingness to participate in rehabilitation programs were often granted reduced prison sentences. States largely abandoned this case-by-case approach to crime and passed tougher drug laws and mandatory-minimum sentencing laws, which quickly filled prison cells throughout the 1980s and 1990s. Most of the criminals sentenced to prison are minority males between the ages of thirty-five and forty-four. The Bureau of Justice Statistics reports that "together, blacks (39%) and Hispanics (18%) constituted a majority of those who had ever served time in prison. . . . Whites accounted for 39% of all those ever incarcerated in 2001, down from 51% in 1974." Many of these offenders come from poor urban communities where family dissolution is common. Explains journalist Carrie Conaway, "Inmates . . . tend to come from troubled homes. Only about 40 percent lived with both parents growing up, and 17 percent lived in a foster home or other institution at some time in their youth. . . . More than a quarter had parents who abused drugs or alcohol, and almost all have a history of abusing alcohol or illegal drugs themselves."

Low educational attainment is also a pervasive problem among inmates. According to the Center on Crime, Communities, and Culture, 19 percent of adult inmates are illiterate—they cannot read, write, or do basic math—compared with 4 percent of the general U.S. population. Another 40 percent of inmates suffer from functional illiteracy and would have trouble filling out a job application, for instance, or composing a letter. Over 70 percent of inmates are high school dropouts. Prior to incarceration, most offenders have been confined to unskilled, low-wage jobs like fast-food server, messenger, or day laborer—jobs that provide no health benefits and leave employees vulnerable to lay-offs. Says Conaway, "Only half [of U.S. inmates] held a full-time job prior to incarceration. . . . [Seventy] percent earned $20,000 or less per year before their incarceration." As Ellen Mason, a manager of prisoner reentry programs in Boston asserts, "For most of these guys, their life up until prison has been a series of failures—failure in their family, failure in school, failure in employment, failure in their interpersonal relationships."

Critics are dismayed that prisons are doing little to improve the basic education and job skills of inmates, trouble spots that may contribute to prisoner recidivism. Burdened with enormous prison populations, states have shifted funds once earmarked for prisoner rehabilitation programs into prison construction and maintenance. In 2001 the Bureau of Justice Statistics reported that only 6 percent of the $22 billion spent on state penitentiaries in 1996 was allocated for rehabilitation programs. Contends journalist Ayelish McGarvey, "The tough-on-crime policies of the 1980s and '90s . . . corroded many prisons' rehabilitative capacities. Various interventions—including drug treatment, vocational training and basic education—have been shown to reduce recidivism, but such programs have been cut . . . nonetheless."

Reintegration into life on the outside presents a formidable challenge for prisoners who have received little or no preparation during their incarceration. According to Alan Elsner, "Most inmates leave prison with no money and few prospects. They may get $25 and a bus ticket if they are lucky. Studies have found that within a year of release, 60 percent of ex-inmates remain unemployed." With limited oversight from overwhelmed parole officers, many ex-cons return to urban neighborhoods where drug abuse, crime, and unemployment are prevalent. The Urban Institute, a social policy think tank, maintains that large numbers of former prisoners "are increasingly concentrated in a relatively small number of communities that already encounter enormous social and economic disadvantage." A prison record makes finding a job in a tight labor market difficult. Criminologist Robert Freeman contends that "employers generally prefer other workers to ex-offenders. Some employers cannot legally hire persons with criminal records for some jobs. Other employers eschew ex-offenders for fear that customers or other workers would sue them if the ex-offender harmed them during work activities." In some cases, returning prisoners lack basic identification such as a driver's license or social security card, delaying their ability to apply for work. Prolonged unemployment may tempt ex-cons back into drug abuse and association with their former partners in crime.

Housing is also a stumbling block to reintegration. In some states, felons are prohibited from holding credit cards, which makes renting a room or an apartment difficult, and staying with family members for an extended period may not be an option. Complains the daughter of ex-con Jean Sanders, "He needs us more than we need him. . . . I've been accustomed to living my life without a father, and now he wants a big welcome-home party." If turned out by their families, ex-cons may end up homeless and resort to crime to survive. Journalist Amanda Ripley contends that "the looming fear is that [ex-cons] . . . will boost crime again, just as their incarceration helped bring it down. Already, crime increases in Boston, Chicago and Los Angeles have been at least partly blamed on their return."

Aware that inmates are not getting the help they need to succeed upon release, criminologists have started to rethink the "cold turkey" approach to prisoner reentry. Urban Institute researchers Jeremy Travis, Amy L. Solomon, and Michelle Waul recommend that inmates participate in structured, prerelease programs that will serve as a short-term bridge during the transition period from inmate to free citizen. These programs can help inmates secure employment, receive substance-abuse treatment, and reestablish family and community ties prior to their release. Travis, Solomon, and Waul contend that "pre-release preparations coupled with follow-up on the outside (via parole, nonprofit community organizations, faith institutions, family, or friends) might reduce the risk of recidivism or drug relapse and improve the odds of successful reintegration after release."

A few jurisdictions are already experimenting with prerelease programs. In Chicago, Adult Transition Centers (ATCs) have been set up by the nonprofit Safer Foundation for the Illinois Department of Corrections. ATCs are residential work-release programs to which inmates serving sentences at Illinois prisons can apply. Once accepted, inmates attend basic education and job training classes and take cognitive tests. Counselors then find inmates suitable jobs with outside companies, where they work a full day and return to the ATC after work hours. According to journalist McGarvey, residential ATCs cost $2,000 less per year than regular incarceration, since a portion of inmate earnings are used to offset program costs. ATCs also show promise in reducing recidivism: Once their prison sentences are over, most ATC inmates are fully employed, have money saved, and enjoy the continued support of job counselors should they need it.

America faces a daunting challenge reintegrating the hundreds of thousands of people incarcerated since the mid-1970s back into society. Providing incarcerated Americans with the education and support networks they need to succeed may go a long way toward reducing recidivism and improve the lives of ex-cons such as Jean Sanders. If transition centers prove successful, a large segment of the population can move out of a cycle of crime and incarceration toward a more promising future of economic independence. *Current Controversies: Prisons* provides a wide array of opinions on the prison system, including the role of rehabilitation programs in reducing recidivism rates.

Chapter 1

Has Society Benefited from More Prisons?

CURRENT CONTROVERSIES

Chapter Preface

The number of adults incarcerated in U.S. prisons rose from 216,000 in 1974 to 1,319,000 in 2001, according to the Bureau of Justice Statistics. In addition, another 700,000 offenders are serving time in city and county jails, bringing the total number of incarcerated Americans to more than 2 million as of spring 2004. To accommodate so many prisoners, jurisdictions have constructed hundreds of new prisons in mostly rural communities at a cost of billions of dollars.

America's prison boom began in the mid-1970s as state governments responded to public dissatisfaction with light prison sentences. The crime reduction efforts of the 1960s had emphasized prisoner rehabilitation; judges and parole boards were granted the discretion to reward promising inmates with shorter sentences or early release. Both criminologists and the public came to regard this "soft-hearted" approach to crime as a failure. Explains Eli Lehrer, a columnist for *National Review* magazine, "In the early 1970s, . . . polls showed huge increases in Americans' fear of crime." No longer willing to give criminals a second chance, states introduced mandatory sentencing policies. Repeat offenders and criminals convicted of certain crimes, particularly the possession of illicit drugs, were sentenced to inflexible prison terms, precluding judicial mitigation.

Proponents of increased incarceration rates argue that locking up more criminals has been the driving force behind falling crime rates, which by 2000 had reached historic lows in big cities like New York. Contends Lehrer, "Locking up criminals for longer periods of time has proven one of America's most effective anticrime strategies. . . . As incarceration rates rose, crime fell." Not only does incarceration incapacitate criminals who would otherwise be out on the streets committing more crimes, it has a deterrent effect as well, dissuading criminals from risking a turn in the "steel hotel."

Other observers hold a less positive view of using prisons as a crime-fighting tool. Marc Mauer of the Sentencing Project, a criminal-justice reform organization, asserts that the prison system has expanded out of all proportion with the number of serious crimes being committed. Changes in sentencing policies have merely cast a wider net, throwing thousands of low-level, nonviolent offenders into prison, he claims. Contends Mauer, "During the period 1980–1996 . . . changes in crime explained only 12% of the prison rise, while changes in sentencing policy accounted for 88% of the increase." Critics like Mauer decry the harmful consequences that mass imprisonment is having on American society, from increased unemployment to family dissolution.

Whether incarceration is a just means to reduce crime is debated in the following chapter. With so many prisons being built and maintained, determining how effective and fair they are has enormous implications for society.

Increased Incarceration Has Reduced Crime

by Ilana Mercer

About the author: *Ilana Mercer is a columnist for WorldNetDaily.com, an on-line magazine. She is also the author of* Broad Sides: One Woman's Clash with a Corrupt Culture.

Anti-incarceration activists are doing a great deal of breast beating over the number of inmates in the U.S. prison system—there were 2,166,260 at year end 2002.

Their emotional statements, such as that "the United States currently imprisons more of its population than any other nation," suggest that all the imprisoned have somehow been aggrieved and aggressed against—and that public policy should aim at reducing prison population *per se*.

But to go ballistic simply because the incarceration figure strikes one as "excessively" large is senseless. And out of context.

Getting Tough Works

It so happens that in the heyday of liberal "alternatives to incarceration"—the mid-1960s through the 1970s—crime rates doubled and tripled. Then something interesting happened: states and the federal government began to get tough, ending early-release programs, limiting parole, passing "truth in sentencing" and "three strikes" laws to up the ante against violent and repeat felons.

The result? Crime rates have plunged, across the board. To take just one category, the Bureau of Justice Statistics [BJS] confirms that the homicide rate, which in 1980 peaked at 10.2 per 100,000 population, has finally "declined sharply, reaching 5.5 per 100,000 by 2000." According to Frank J. Murray's *Washington Times* October [2003] report on the topic, murder has hit a 40-year low.

Contrary to the claims of MotherJones.com, the beloved source reference for liberals and radical-chic libertarians, more violent and repeat offenders are be-

Ilana Mercer, "The Criminal's Theoretical Enablers," www.WorldNetDaily.com, January 9, 2004.

17

ing incarcerated and for longer. Which means that they are no longer free to commit crimes.

Contrary to the propaganda of such anti-punishment ideologues, our prisons aren't loaded with choir boys. The BJS reports that "Of the 272,111 persons released from prisons in 15 states in 1994, an estimated 67.5 percent were rearrested for a felony or serious misdemeanor within 3 years, 46.9 percent were reconvicted, and 25.4 percent resentenced to prison for a new crime." These 272,111 discharged offenders accounted for nearly 4,877,000 arrest charges over their recorded careers.

> *"By locking up more . . . sociopaths for longer terms, society is much safer."*

In other words, the overwhelming majority of incarcerated felons deserve to be there. And by locking up more such sociopaths for longer terms, society is much safer.

Moreover, justice is done: The consequences to the criminal are now much more proportionate to the harm he does to his victims.

Flawed Liberal Theories

Anti-incarceration theorists, among whom are assorted liberals and libertarian anarchists, point out quite correctly that crimes are committed against individuals and not against the amorphous entity called "society." Solutions, they say, should thus focus on making criminals pay restitution to their victims.

It used to be that the cause *du jour* among libertarians was to reduce prison population by freeing innocent people whose activities, lawful by natural-law standards, the state had criminalized. Now their aim, it seems, is to reduce the involvement of the state at any costs, even if it means freeing guilty offenders.

And in their quest to get the state out of the loop by emptying jails, anti-incarceration "individualists" have embraced a convenient collectivist argument. Imprisonment has "social costs"—costs to the same *collective* that they deny when defining the parameters of crime.

If we are going to be "methodological individualists," let's be even-handed about it, shall we?

When more dangerous offenders are incarcerated, more innocent individuals (not "society") incur fewer costs. When fewer violent criminals are apprehended, more innocent individuals (not "society") are harmed. If innocent individuals are incarcerated, they (and not "society") are harmed as well as many other individuals like them.

Moreover, anarchist libertarians cunningly, incorrectly and condescendingly conflate punishment with vengeance, and restitution with justice. And so we are treated to facile flimflam such as that "the desire for vengeance" (read punishment) cannot become "the foundation of jurisprudence." By this verbal manipulation, these "thinkers" disingenuously advance a definition of justice that precludes incarceration, and equates it *only* with restitution.

While no one would argue against compelling criminals to work for their victims, libertarian anarchists essentially want to see punishment *replaced* by a system of financial restitution. But in cases (and there are many) where criminals can't remotely repay victims for the harm done (especially in violent crimes), this means the consequences to the criminal won't be remotely proportionate. In effect, by rejecting proportionate punishment for what is usually disproportionately paltry "restitution," libertarian anarchists are endorsing systematic *injustice.*

For example, libertarian theorists like Bruce Benson uphold primitive societies as a model for how judicial reform must proceed. In these societies, writes Benson in [the 1996 essay] "Restitution in Theory and Practice," the emphasis was on the victim's right to expect restoration from their victimizers but *not* to exact punishment. By this, he means: *Not* to expect proportionate justice.

Benson effects a bogus bifurcation. Victims, for whom he presumes to speak, are said to want restitution from their victimizers. Justice for victims he then equates only with financial restitution. It is only the state, you see, that wants punishment, incapacitation and deterrence, all of which—if we accept Benson's claims—the typical victim of crime isn't enthusiastic about.

The Necessity of Punishment

While no one would argue against restitution—where possible—I have never heard a victim of crime suggest that a financial settlement with her rapist is far preferable to having the scum bag removed from "society." (Forgive my unelevated sentiments—it's the Old Testament in me.)

In fact, to listen to victims of crime is to know that libertarian anarchists are proffering formulations that fit the demands of theory, not humanity.

I suppose it is hypothetically possible that, as Benson and others assert, medieval England, Ireland, Iceland, even Somali tribes are worthy exemplars of how we ought to settle disputes today. It is also equally plausible that the average victim has no sense of justice, and desperately needs the postgraduate cleverness of the libertarian anarchist to help her gain perspective.

> "If the necessary precautions are not taken to incapacitate [known] attackers, other members of the community might suffer."

But beneath the clouds of platonic theorizing, and back on *terra firma*, victims of crime almost always demand punishment that fits the crime, and express a fear that if the necessary precautions are not taken to incapacitate their attackers, other members of the community might suffer as they have.

This is not revenge; it is common sense.

In his seminal [1994] essay, "Crime and Moral Retribution," Robert James Bidinotto provides a definition of just *retribution* as opposed to *revenge.* "Revenge," he writes, "means the carrying out of a bitter desire to injure another for a wrong done to oneself or to those who seem a part of oneself. By contrast, though, retribution suggests just or deserved punishment, often without personal motives, for some evil done."

Bidinotto, [editor of the 1994 anthology] *Criminal Justice? The Legal System Versus Individual Responsibility*, refers to liberal and libertarian enablers of criminals as "the Excuse-Making Industry." He points out that a legal system that imposes proportionate, retributive justice may well incorporate restitution into its scheme of punishments—but that this can't work in reverse.

"Criminals are notoriously unproductive, while causing tremendous harm," he says. "Expecting them to be able to repay victims is simply absurd. Thus, relying on restitution alone means that the worst offenders will never have to pay a price that begins to match the damages they cause. They will learn that, for them, 'crime pays.'"

Still, for the sake of argument, let's presume that our rape victim—she's a liberal or libertarian penal abolitionist—forfeits punishment in favor of payoff. Her rapist, she argues, offended against her alone. Since he has settled the score (fat chance), he must go free.

She may find this satisfactory, but what of the rest of us? Again, one doesn't have to be "methodological individualist" to know that many besides her face a clear and present danger from the "paid-up" rapist. Recidivism rates among criminals more than demonstrate this plain point.

In such cases, restitution should be *added* to incarceration, not substituted for it. Justice for all demands no less.

The Threat of Incarceration Deters Criminal Behavior

by Morgan Reynolds

About the author: *Morgan Reynolds is a professor of economics at Texas A&M University and a senior fellow with the National Center for Policy Analysis, a conservative think tank.*

Editor's Note: The following viewpoint was originally given as testimony before Congress on October 2, 2000.

I appreciate the invitation to testify before the subcommittee today on the question of whether or not punishment works to reduce crime.

The answer is obvious to most Americans—yes, of course punishment reduces crime. Punishment converts criminal activity from a paying proposition to a nonpaying proposition, at least sometimes, and people respond accordingly. We all are aware of how similar incentives work in our lives, for example, choosing whether or not to drive faster than the law allows. (How many of us in this room, for example, have run afoul of law enforcement on a traffic charge?) Incentives matter, including the risks we are willing to run. This is only a commonsense observation about how people choose to behave. Yet controversy over the very existence of a deterrence and incapacitation effect of incarceration has raged in elite circles.

Incarceration's Effect on Crime

The first duty of a scientist, it's been said, is to point out the obvious. The logic of deterrence is pretty obvious, but I must point to evidence too, which is overwhelming, for the negative impact of punishment on crime. Evidence ranges from simple facts to sophisticated statistical and econometric studies.

Even experts who disagree with each other about some aspects of criminal justice are in agreement about deterrence. For example, when *Forbes* magazine asked John Lott, senior research scholar at Yale Law School and author of *More*

Morgan Reynolds, testimony before the House Subcommittee on Crime, Committee on the Judiciary, Washington, DC, October 2, 2000.

Guns, Less Crime, "Why the recent drop in crime?" he responded, "Lots of reasons—increases in arrest rates, conviction rates, prison sentence lengths." And Daniel Nagin, a Carnegie-Mellon University professor of public policy who co-authored an article in the *Journal of Legal Studies* critical of Lott's work on concealed carry laws, says in *The Handbook of Crime and Punishment*, Oxford, 1998, "The combined deterrent and incapacitation effect generated by the collective actions of the police, courts, and prison system is very large."

In sharp contrast to the situation ten years ago, experts who assert the contrary are fighting a rearguard action. Crime rates have fallen 30 percent over the last decade while the

> *"The threat of bad consequences . . . is vital to secure human rights to life and property against predation."*

prison and jail population doubled to two million. Most people are able to connect these dots (*The New York Times* aside), and even the academy has caught on. As German philosopher Arthur Schopenhauer said, truth passes through three stages, first, it is ridiculed, second, it is violently opposed, and third, it is accepted as being self-evident.

Simple, everyday facts about crime are easy to explain from an incentive-based perspective and hard to explain from any other perspective:

- The cops are never around when you need them (because criminals are not stupid enough to commit crimes in front of the cops).
- When the police participate in a labor strike or "sick out,"crime sprees break out (and in the aftermath of natural disasters, looting runs riot unless the [National] Guard is called up).
- Prison and jail officials daily manage two million less-than-model citizens living in close quarters with few incidents (order is sustained because inmates heed incentives).

Given the avarice of man, the hard reality is that the threat of bad consequences, including public retribution posed by the legal system, is vital to secure human rights to life and property against predation. If men were angels, as James Madison said, we'd have no need of government.

The sad part about prisons is that the most effective crime reducer is the intact family. But government policies have gone far to undermine the family, intensifying the crime problem (welfare, taxes, no-fault divorce, etc.). As internal restraints (character, morality, virtue) degrade, we lamentably rely on external restraints to protect civilization, at least in the short run. As Edmund Burke, English political philosopher, said, "Society cannot exist unless a controlling power upon will and appetite be placed somewhere, and the less of it there is within, the more there must be without . . . men of intemperate minds cannot be free. Their passions forge their fetters."

Criminality is purposeful human behavior. The testimony of criminals provides perhaps our strongest evidence that, in the vast majority of cases, lawbreakers reason and act like other human beings (also a fundamental proposition in the justice system). Criminologists Richard Wright and Scott Decker interviewed 105 active, nonincarcerated residential burglars in St. Louis, Mo. Burglar No. 013 said, "After my eight years for robbery, I told myself then I'll never do another robbery because I was locked up with so many guys that was doin' 25 to 30 years for robbery and I think that's what made me stick to burglaries, because I had learned that a crime committed with a weapon will get you a lot of time."

Burglars also choose their targets by considering both risks and rewards. For example:

- Burglars avoid neighborhoods that are heavily patrolled or aggressively policed: "You got to stay away from where the police ride real tough."
- Nine out of 10 burglars say they *always* avoid breaking into an occupied residence: "I rather for the police to catch me vs. a person catching me breaking in their house because the person will kill you. Sometimes the police will tell you, 'You lucky we came before they did.'"
- Realistically enough, burglars perceive the chance of being apprehended for a given break-in as extremely slim, partly because they efficiently search the master bedroom first (cash, jewelry, guns) and do not linger inside the target.

Only after World War II did scholars begin to statistically study the effects of deterrence. Today a large body of scholarly literature generally confirms the value of punishment in the prevention of crime.

> *"The [United States] has had to imprison more people in recent years because it failed to do so earlier."*

Perhaps the most widely cited is Isaac Ehrlich's 1973 study of punishment and deterrence in the *Journal of Political Economy.* Using state data for 1940, 1950 and 1960, Ehrlich found that crime varied inversely with the probability of prison and the average time served.

More recently, University of Chicago economist Steven Levitt estimated that for each 10 percent rise in a state's prison population, robberies fall 7 percent, assault and burglary shrink 4 percent each, auto theft and larceny decline 3 percent each, rape falls 2½ percent and murder drops 1½ percent. On average, 10 to 15 nondrug felonies are eliminated for each additional prisoner locked up, saving social costs estimated at $53,900, well in excess of the $30,000 it costs annually to incarcerate a prisoner.

Deterrence vs. Incapacitation

Scholars also ask which provides the greater deterrent, certainty or severity of punishment? One provocative study involving prisoners and college students came down firmly on the side of certainty. When tested, both groups responded in virtually identical terms. Prisoners could identify their financial self-interest in an experimental setting as well as students could. However, in their decision making, prisoners were much more sensitive to changes in certainty than in severity of punishment. In terms of real-world application, the authors of the study speculate that long prison terms are likely to be more impressive to lawmakers than lawbreakers.

Supporting evidence for this viewpoint comes from a National Academy of Sciences panel which claimed that a 50 percent increase in the probability of incarceration prevents about twice as much violent crime as a 50 percent increase in the average term of incarceration.

Nonetheless, severity of punishment also remains crucial for deterrence. "A prompt and certain slap on the wrist," criminologist Ernest van den Haag wrote, "helps little." Or, as Milwaukee Judge Ralph Adam Fine wrote, "We keep our hands out of a flame because it hurt the very first time (not the second, fifth or 10th time) we touched the fire."

Distinguishing between the deterrent and incapacitation effects of prison is empirically difficult, but economists Daniel Kessler and Levitt cleverly separate the two using California data on sentence enhancements. Proposition 8, which imposed longer sentences for a selected group of crimes, reduced these crimes by 4 percent within one year of passage and by 8 percent within three years after passage. These immediate effects are consistent with deterrence since there is no additional incapacitation impact in the short run.

If the United States, with so many people in prison, has one of the world's highest crime rates, doesn't this imply that prison does not work? Scholar Charles Murray has examined this question and concluded that the answer is no. Instead, the nation has had to imprison more people in recent years because it failed to do so earlier (the war on drugs also plays a role). Murray compared the record of the risk of imprisonment in England to that in the United States.

In England the risk of going to prison for committing a crime fell by about 80 percent over a period of 40 years and the English crime rate gradually rose.

"There is a close connection between lack of punishment and the forming of criminal habits."

By contrast, the risk of going to prison in the U.S. fell by 64 percent in just 10 years starting in 1961 and the U.S. crime rate shot up.

In the United States, it was not a matter of crimes increasing so fast that the rate of imprisonment could not keep up. Rather, the rate of imprisonment fell first by deliberate policy decisions. By the time the U.S. began incarcerating more criminals in the mid-1970s, huge increases were required to bring the risk of imprisonment up to the crime rate. It is more difficult to reestablish a high rate of imprisonment after the crime rate has escalated than to maintain a high risk of imprisonment from the outset, Murray concluded. We've experienced the same phenomenon in Texas, where crime rocketed up in the 1980s while punishment plunged.

However, both the U.S. and Texas experiences showed that it is possible for imprisonment to stop a rising crime rate and then gradually begin to push it down. The American crime rate peaked in 1980, a few years after the risk of imprisonment reached its nadir. Since then, as the risk of imprisonment has increased, with few exceptions the rates of serious crimes have retreated in fits and starts to levels of 20 or more years ago. My own research for the NCPA [National Center for Policy Analysis] shows that expected punishment has had an inverse correlation with crime rates for both Texas and the nation.

The Challenge of Juveniles

Juvenile offenders, due to their youth and immaturity, pose a special challenge to the criminal justice system. In the past, many judges and social workers have argued for less stringent treatment of such offenders, with "prevention" taking precedence over detention. The focus tends to be on so-called root causes, rehabilitation and nonpunitive approaches. Yet there is a close connection between lack of punishment and the forming of criminal habits. Recent studies note the effectiveness of punishment for juveniles, not just adults. Between 1980 and 1993 juvenile crime rose alarmingly, and as the states toughened their approach during the 1990s, it declined just as steeply.

Likewise, in his study of criminal justice in England, Charles Murray found that in 1954 the system operated on the assumption that the best way to keep crime down was to intervene early and sternly. Crime was very low, and the number of youths picked up by the police went down by about half as children matured from their early to their late teens. Today, however, a widespread assumption in England (as in the United States) is that youthful offenders need patience more than punishment. England's traditionally low crime rate is now very high, and the number of youths picked up by the police roughly triples from the early to the late teens.

The need to hold the individual juvenile criminal responsible for his actions does not make incarceration the sole option. For example, Anne L. Schneider found in six random-assignment experiments involving 876 adjudicated (convicted) delinquents in six American cities that victim restitution and incarceration both lowered reoffending while probation did not. Victim restitution meant monetary restitution, community service or work to repay the victims.

Rehabilitation's Shortcomings

Believers in rehabilitation regard punishment as primitive or counterproductive. For example, Alvin Bronstein, former executive director of the American Civil Liberties Union's National Prison Project, contended that releasing half the nation's prisoners would have little or no effect on the U.S. crime rate.

A major obstacle for such sunny optimism is the existence of what might be called the criminal personality. Perhaps the most important work on this subject is the three-volume study by the late Samuel Yochelson, a physician, and Stanton Samenow, a practicing psychologist. After interviewing hundreds of criminals and their relatives and acquaintances, the two researchers concluded that criminals (1) have control over what they do, freely choosing evil over good, (2) have distinct personalities, described in detail as deceitful, egotistical, myopic and violent and (3) make specific errors in thinking (52 such errors are identified).

Yochelson and Samenow assert that the criminal must resolve to change and accept responsibility for his own behavior. Hardened criminals can reform themselves, but Samenow estimates that only 10 percent would

> *"Despite . . . calls for a 'better way,' what criminals need most is evidence that their crimes do not pay."*

choose to do so. He avoids the word "rehabilitation" when describing chronic criminals: "When you think of how these people react, how their patterns go back to age 3 or 4, there isn't anything to rehabilitate."

Careful studies of well-intended but soft-headed programs continue to find little payoff. In the case of street gang crime, Professor Malcolm Klein found that typical liberal-based gang interventions have failed to manifest much utility. They appeal to our best instincts, but are too indirect, too narrow or else produce boomerang effects by producing increased gang cohesiveness.

The truth is that changing criminal behavior by means other than deterrence is always problematical. A comprehensive scientific evaluation of hundreds of previous studies and prevention programs funded by the Justice Department found that "some programs work, some don't, and some may even increase crime." The report was prepared by the University of Maryland's Department of Criminology and Criminal Justice for the Justice Department and mandated by Congress. Still, too little is known and the report calls for 10 percent of all federal funding for these programs to be spent on independent evaluations of the impact of prevention programs.

Just Deserts

Public opinion strongly supports the increased use of prisons to give criminals their just deserts. The endorsement of punishment is relatively uniform across social groups. More than three-quarters of the public see punishment as the primary justification for sentencing. More than 70 percent believe that incapacitation is the only sure way to prevent future crimes, and more than three-quarters believe that the courts are too easy on criminals. Three-quarters favor the death penalty for murder.

Still, the public holds out some hope for rehabilitation, too. About 60 percent express hope that services like psychological counseling, training and education inside prison will correct personal shortcomings. Such sentiments are more likely to be expressed on behalf of young offenders than adults, and by nonwhite respondents.

Despite continuing calls for a "better way," what criminals need most is evidence that their crimes do not pay. Neither criminals nor the rest of us "drive a car 100 miles an hour toward a brick wall, because we know what the consequences will be," as author Robert Bidinotto puts it. Punishment flat works. It's unpleasant and expensive, yes, but among other virtues, it supplies the convict with a major incentive to reform. Even career criminals often give up crime because they don't want to go back to prison. The old prescription that punishment be swift, certain and severe is affirmed by modern social science.

As expected punishment plunged during the 1960s and 1970s, crime rose astronomically. When expected punishment began rising in the 1980s and 1990s, crime leveled of and began falling. With the well-publicized success of nononsense police tactics like those in New York City, few observers today doubt that the criminal justice system can have a major impact on crime. Does that mean that everything has been done perfectly over the last decade? No, there is plenty of room for improvement in the future, but that is another subject.

Imprisonment Is a Socially Just Response to Crime

by Lowell Ponte

About the author: *Conservative commentator Lowell Ponte hosts a nationally syndicated talk-radio program and is a frequent contributor to FrontPage Mag.com.*

"U.S. Has Highest Adult Imprisonment Rate in the World," screamed the headline of a story in Monday's [August 11, 2003] *Chicago Sun-Times*.

The Justice Department's Bureau of Justice Statistics' new study [*Prevalence of Imprisonment in the U.S. Population, 1974–2001*], this newspaper reported, reveals that about one of every 37 U.S. adults either was imprisoned at the end of 2001 or at one time had done time in a state or federal prison. This adds up to about 5.6 million people, approximately 2.7 of every 100 American adults.

Misconstruing American Justice

"Stone walls do not a prison make, nor iron bars a cage," wrote 17th Century poet Richard Lovelace. A prison can be many things.

Entire Marxist nations such as Communist China, North Korea and Cuba are gigantic prisons whose millions of inmates are denied human rights, civil liberties, economic freedom, and above all the right to leave.

Why do Leftist journalists never mention that the 2.7 percent rate of incarceration in the United States is vastly lower than the 99+ percent enslavement of the populace common to Communist lands?

What instead stimulates the Pavlovian salivation of such journalists seems to be their eagerness to use this study as yet another stick with which to hit and harm the United States. Because we imprison a larger percentage of our population than any other nation, the reporting implies, we are somehow less free or more violent (or both) than any other nation.

The study predicts that our courts will soon be imprisoning a larger and larger share of Americans. Of those born in 2001, it speculates, one of every 15 will spend time behind bars.

Even worse, the reporting implies, is that, in America, Lady Justice may be blindfolded but seems not to be colorblind. Is racism the reason why so great a difference exists in the racial composition of the U.S. prison population?

In 2001, the study found, nearly one of every six African-American men are current or former prisoners, as were one of every 13 Hispanic males and one of every 38 whites.

In the highest risk 35–44 year age group, today 22 percent of black males are or have been prisoners, compared to 10 percent of Hispanic males and 3.5 percent of white males.

"Liberals tend to see racism as the cause of [the racial] disparity [in U.S. prisons]."

But for children born in 2001, the study projects that the rising rate of imprisonment will cause approximately one of every three black males, one of every six Hispanic males, and one of every 17 whites to spend part of their lives in state or federal prison.

(Asian-American and Jewish prison rates are too low to be a significant factor in this research. Women have recently doubled their proportion among prisoners, but their lifetime chance of going to prison is projected to be only 1.8 percent, compared to an overall male likelihood of 11.3 percent.)

False Assertions of Racism

Liberals tend to see racism as the cause of this disparity. The FBI long encouraged police to pay attention to higher-than-average black crime statistics, their argument goes, and this leads to more profiling of African-Americans as potential criminals to be watched. This becomes a self-fulfilling prophecy, with more surveillance of blacks and a dollop of cop racism producing more black arrests and convictions.

Inside the Leftist mind plays the 1938 movie *Angels with Dirty Faces.* Two juvenile delinquent kids are chased by the cops, and both try to escape by jumping a fence. One makes it, escapes punishment, and becomes a Roman Catholic priest played by Pat O'Brien. The other gets grabbed before he clears the fence, gets sent to learn crime from other delinquents in reform school, and becomes a gangster played by James Cagney.

The only difference between them, liberals believe, is that one got caught and was sent spiraling downward—as so many African-Americans are by prison experience and its blot on their job resume—while the other equally criminal youngster outran police and became a veritable saint. The politically correct subtext is that we are beneficiaries or victims of fate or luck or other forces beyond our control.

Some truth exists in the argument that the higher arrest and conviction rates for blacks prompts police to expect in future what such statistics show. Some truth is found in the idea that we are a mixed society bringing together many cultures and races that only partly understand each other, and this leads to more potential social conflict than would exist in nations that are racial-ethnic mono-cultures of conformity such as Sweden.

But honesty compels us to speak a far more Politically Incorrect truth. Although two of every three African-Americans is hard-working, honest, law-abiding, moral and Middle Class, the remaining third is part of an economic underclass.

This minority subclass for the most part lives in Inner City social environments. Its sons, nearly 70 percent of whom are born and raised by single mothers, have as their male role models the local pimp, drug dealer, and poverty pimp politician.

The politics of this environment are steeped in both racism and classism, with demagogues like the Reverend Jesse Jackson making themselves rich by preaching that these neighborhoods' problems come not from their own irresponsibility but from those who are white and rich.

The voodoo politics Rev. Jackson and his ilk offer is to tell their followers to vote for Democrats, who will then use government power to confiscate what others have earned and redistribute this wealth in welfare checks, government jobs, and other goodies to those in the Inner City.

Legitimizing Crime

Such welfarist politics legitimize violence and theft. They tell Inner City residents that they are entitled to take the wealth others have earned. Should we be surprised that many of these people decide to eliminate the government middle-man (and the 80 percent cut the government has taken for itself, its politicians and operatives, during schemes like the $7+ trillion "War on Poverty")? If rich white folks are evil and deserve to have their wealth taken away, why not just take it yourself?

The politics of class hatred and wealth redistribution—the bread and butter of the Democratic Party and its slave masters like Rev. Jackson—might be the single biggest cause of minority crime in America. By legitimizing theft, it promotes theft. By legitimizing violence and hatred, it stimulates violence and hatred.

Rev. Jackson himself unwittingly confirmed this years ago, telling one interviewer that one dark night walking down a street in Washington, D.C., he was frightened to hear footsteps approaching. Then, said Rev. Jackson, he felt "relieved" when he saw that the walkers overtaking and passing him were white.

"The Politically Incorrect truth is that African-Americans . . . commit a disproportionate share of crime."

The Politically Incorrect truth is that African-Americans are a disproportionately large part of America's prison population in part because—take a deep breath—they commit a disproportionate share of crime, violent as well as self-inflicted "victimless" crime.

The biggest cause of this is not only racism but welfarism—the concoction and perpetuation of a subculture that makes excuses for criminal behavior, condones theft, and practices a Leftist class hatred and envy as virulent as any racism ever preached by the Ku Klux Klan.

> *"A disproportionate share of crime victims have also been minorities, who are now safer in their own neighborhoods."*

"Don't you understand, Lowell," a famous Leftist intellectual once told me over drinks, "that welfare is the price we pay for keeping the poor *in their place*." Their place, the ruling Democratic Party elite believes, is in helplessness and government dependency down on the welfare plantation where their votes can be harvested every time elections come.

Yet by using minority votes to gain the political power to rob the rich, but then sharing only crumbs of that stolen swag with the poor, Democrats like Rev. Jackson have caused widespread minority despair, frustration, incipient violence and the drug use that also puts a disproportionate number of African-Americans into prison.

And now so many have been and will be sent to prison that, unless the Democratic Party's crusade to change laws succeeds, four million prisoners and former prisoners will remain unable to vote. In 12 states a convicted felon loses the vote for the rest of his or her life. A disproportionate share of these will be African-Americans, the minority on which the Democratic Party depends now for nearly one out of five of its votes.

Safer Streets

Why is the proportion of our population in prison increasing? The Federal Government has been moving to mandatory sentencing laws, taking the discretion to be lenient out of the hands of Leftist judges. States have also been adopting "three strikes and you're out" laws that send repeat criminals to prison, even when the third crime demonstrating their criminal mentality is as trivial as stealing a piece of pizza or a bicycle.

"In my view, our resources are being misspent," U.S. Supreme Court Justice Anthony Kennedy last Saturday [August 9, 2003] told the American Bar Association. "Our punishments are too severe and our sentences are too long. . . . In all too many cases, mandatory minimum sentences are unjust."

But do not expect Congress to roll back its new policies. Since 1995 the federal prison population has grown by 41 percent and—surprise, surprise—with these criminals off the streets the crime rate in the last decade has gone down by about 50 percent.

A disproportionate share of crime victims have also been minorities, who are now safer in their own neighborhoods.

One potential path to reducing America's prison population was signed into law Monday [August 11, 2003] by Illinois Governor Rod Blagojevich. It will require Chicago Public Schools, starting January 1, 2004, to identify (by techniques not yet defined) students considered at risk for committing future crimes. Yes, it sounds like the recent movie *Minority Report* about people arrested on the accusation of psychics that they will commit crimes in the future.

Under this new law, these potentially criminal students will then be taken on tours of a state prison in a kind of "scared straight" effort to show them where antisocial behavior might lead. (Too bad these kids have [former U.S. president and first lady] Bill and Hillary Clinton and their Leftist elite co-conspirators as counter-examples of how crime pays if you are powerful, crooked and brazen enough.)

We have come a long way from school kids taking field trips to fields or dairy farms. We have even left behind the *film noir* ugly images in black and white of crime and prison life.

At least in *Angels with Dirty Faces* the gangster Jimmy Cagney honors his attending priest friend Pat O'Brien by pretending to be a whimpering coward and weakling when he is taken to the prison execution chamber. In this way he makes a last redemptive gesture to show youngsters who hear reports of his death that a life of crime does not pay and should be avoided.

Prisons have much to teach us. Perhaps we should consider field trips behind bars not just for antisocial youngsters but for all students. We have made such places a cornerstone on which our social order rests, every bit as much as are our legislatures or newspapers or classrooms. Experiencing such a place, if only for a few hours as a visitor, should be part of everybody's life education.

The Costs of Prison Expansion Are Warranted

by Gary Aldrich

About the author: *Gary Aldrich is president and founder of the Patrick Henry Center for Individual Liberty, an organization that favors tough-on-crime policies.*

How do we count the many differences between Hard-Left-Liberals and average, normal folks? Fortunately, Liberal publications like the *Washington Post* make the distinction easy to spot.

Hollow Complaints

Consider one headline in a . . . *Washington Post* article, originating from an Associated Press release written by Curt Anderson. Mind you, the AP is also a well-established, highly respected media organization that distributes "news" to thousands of newspapers across the land. That said, their objective decision-makers write, "Number of Prisoners Rises as Crime Drops." They go on to point out that prison costs are rising at a time of "rampant budget shortfalls." You might ask the obvious question, "So what?"

Shall we set violent prisoners free to save money? I guess Hard-Left Liberals think so.

This headline could have been written in many different ways, absent the Hard-Left Liberal slant. For example, "Study Finds that When Crooks are Locked Up, Crime Drops." Or, "Society Safer as Crooks Fill Jail Cells." Another positive option could be, "Number of Crime Victims decreases as Career Criminals are Incarcerated."

Maybe I'm picking a nit here, but I know from my long experience in crime fighting that there is an ever-present support group for hardened criminals which believes that life sentences for third-time offenders are unfair. They are also bothered, for some inexplicable reason, that it costs money to house prisoners in jails.

In fact, this AP story went on to quote several pro-criminal groups who whine that the total cost to our society to house the existing prison population is estimated to be 40 billion dollars. They make a point of mentioning that for cash-strapped state and federal governments, this is money that could best be spent elsewhere, or not spent at all.

The amazing fact about Hard-Left Liberals is that they usually spend money like drunken sailors on shore leave—except when they disagree with a particular cause, like putting hard-core deadly prisoners away for life. The fact that Republicans in general and Conservatives in particular are known as "tough on crime" cannot help the cause of law enforcement supporters. It's become reflexive for the Hard-Left to attack any policy or program that makes the GOP [Republican Party] look good.

It might be good to review the history of our current crime statistics. In 1993, Republicans like Dick Armey and Newt Gingrich made fighting crime a pillar of their 10-point Contract with America. In fact, crime was the #2 issue on their chart. They proposed that if states would build more prisons, the federal government would help fund them—but there was a catch. States that wanted federal dollars had to pass three-time loser laws so career criminals would not be allowed to continue their crime spree.

States lined up for the money and enjoyed the positive voter response they knew would result from safer neighborhoods. They passed the laws and prisons were built and filled. Soon we began to see a decrease in the crime rate, but of course the bleeding hearts were upset that so many were locked up for good. They complained of harsh prison conditions—when everybody knows what that means: The prisoner's video game has shorted out, the free-weight set is not cutting edge, or the cable TV needs repair! As a population, we have become too educated to buy the sad cause of "prisoners' rights."

Incarceration Reduces the Costs of Crime

Harsh prison conditions didn't work, so now the Hard-Left raises the cost issue. What the AP story will not tell you is that before the GOP and the Conservatives insisted that we become tough on crime, the total cost to our society from the crimes being committed—from the burial and hospitalization of the victims, to the cost of the investigations and the insurance now required by everyone to protect themselves against crime—the total costs came to a whopping 100 times the cost of keeping these animals behind bars!

As the man says, "You can pay me now, or later you will pay me much more." Would you rather pay $40 billion now to keep these guys behind bars, or would you like to pay $400 billion later, so bleeding hearts can feel better about themselves?

Reporters working for the AP and editors working for the *Washington Post* are counting on your emotional response so that criminals can have an easier time of it. *Post* editors live in gated communities—the rest of us must defend ourselves against the vicious career criminals who have not yet been caught and put away for good.

Increased Incarceration Has Not Reduced Crime

by Vince Beiser

About the author: *Vince Beiser is senior editor of MotherJones.com, the online journal of liberal commentary affiliated with* Mother Jones *magazine.*

In the heart of Los Angeles, just a few blocks from the downtown commuter hub of Union Station, stands a pair of massive concrete towers. Tinted in bland desert tones of beige and dull rose, the angular, unapologetically functional buildings could be some big corporation's headquarters, or a hospital, or perhaps a research facility. Only the windows—nearly all of them narrow, vertical slits through which nothing can be seen from the outside—give a clue to what the complex really is: the Twin Towers Correctional Facility, which happens to be the world's biggest jail.

Linking the towers is a low-lying structure called the Inmate Reception Center [IRC]. This is the first stop for every inmate taken into custody by the Los Angeles County Sheriff's Department. Each day, as many as 6,000 prisoners pass through the IRC's vast labyrinth of hallways and holding areas. It takes a staff of 800 just to log, sort, and monitor them, from booking and fingerprinting to locking them up in cells crowded with other inmates.

The Surging Prison Population

Local taxpayers spent nearly $400 million to build the Towers in the early '90s because older jails were overflowing with arrestees. The jails, in turn, serve as gateways for the 21 new prisons the state has built since 1980. Over the past two decades, the number of inmates in those prisons has grown sevenfold, to more than 160,000. It cost California taxpayers nearly $5.3 billion to build the new lockups—and it costs another $4.8 billion every year to keep them running.

California is no anomaly; over the last 20 years, the number of prisoners has surged in every state in the country. While the nation's population has grown by only 20 percent, the number of Americans held in local, state, and federal lockups has doubled—and then doubled again. The United States now locks up some two million people. That's far more than ever before, and more than any other country on earth. And the number is still growing.

Most Americans never even see, let alone become ensnared in, the nation's vast correctional system. But the unprecedented prison boom is incurring unprecedented costs—economic, social and ethical—that are being paid, one way or another, by everyone in this country. . . .

How did this happen? How did a nation dedicated to the principle of freedom become the world's leading jailer? The answer has little to do with crime, but much to do with the perception of crime, and how that perception has been manipulated for political gain and financial profit. From state legislatures to the White House, politicians have increasingly turned to tough-on-crime policies as guaranteed vote-getters. That trend has been encouraged by the media, which use the public's fearful fascination with crime to boost ratings, and by private-prison companies, guards' unions, and other interests whose business depends on mass-scale incarceration.

Crime Down, Incarceration Up

Prisons certainly aren't expanding because more crimes are being committed. Since 1980, the national crime rate has meandered down, then up, then down again—but the incarceration rate has marched relentlessly upward every single year. Nationwide, crime rates today are comparable to those of the 1970s, but the incarceration rate is four times higher than it was then. It's not crime that has increased; it's punishment. More people are now arrested for minor offenses, more arrestees are prosecuted, and more of those convicted are given lengthy sentences. Huge numbers of current prisoners are locked up for drug offenses and other transgressions that would not have met with such harsh punishment 20 years ago.

In return for spending so much more on prisons today—a nationwide total of some $46 billion annually—taxpayers might reasonably expect a corresponding drop in crime. But most experts agree that prisons have done little to make communities safer. A . . . study by the University of Texas estimates that while the number of inmates has grown by more than 300 percent since the late 1970s, that growth is responsible for no more than 27 percent of the recent drop in crime. Indeed, many states with the fastest increases in prison populations received no commensurate payback in crime reduction. In West Virginia, for example, the incarceration rate ballooned by 131 percent over the past decade—but crime dropped by only 4 percent. Meanwhile, in neighboring Virginia, incarceration rose just 28 percent, but crime dropped 21 percent.

> *"Experts agree that a combination of . . . factors . . . [has] done far more than incarceration to cut crime."*

Locking up more people only reduces crime if those being locked up are serious criminals, experts say. "If it's a serial rapist, that makes an impact on crime," explains Marc Mauer, assistant director of the Sentencing Project, a research and advocacy group based in Washington, D.C. "But if it's a kid selling crack on the corner, that just creates a job opening for someone else." Most experts agree that a combination of other factors, including the until-recently strong economy, more effective policing, and the decline of the crack trade have done far more than incarceration to cut crime.

Roots of the Prison Explosion

The fuse of America's prison explosion was lit in the late 1960s. With a war raging in Vietnam, riots sweeping major cities, and protests roiling college campuses, middle America was hungry for action to restore law and order. In 1968, Congress responded with a major anti-crime bill that doled out millions of dollars to local police and increased the federal government's involvement in local law enforcement. Crime had never been much of an issue in federal politics before, but Richard Nixon made it a central campaign theme that year. Shortly after his election, Nixon added narcotics to the list of America's leading enemies, sounding the call to a national war on drugs. "The abuse of drugs has grown from essentially a local police problem into a serious national threat to

"For politicians, crime pays."

the personal health and safety of millions of Americans," he declared.

Around the same time, states began eliminating the flexibility that judges and parole boards had long exercised in deciding how to punish offenders and when to let them out of prison. Liberals denounced the old system as rife with racial discrimination; conservatives slammed it for being too lenient. Both called for fixed, mandatory sentences for specific crimes. In 1973, New York governor Nelson Rockefeller set a new standard by pushing through what are still some of the nation's harshest sentences for drug crimes, including mandatory 15-year prison terms for possessing small amounts of narcotics. The concept caught on: By now [2001], nearly every state and the federal government have some form of mandatory sentencing.

Mandatory sentencing leaves judges little room to maneuver: Those found guilty are automatically locked up for predetermined amounts of time. "With the power of release taken away from parole authorities, and judge's discretion also removed, it was left by default to the legislatures to set sentencing policy," says Franklin Zimring, a criminologist at the University of California at Berkeley. "Punishment became a political decision." Even archconservative U.S. Supreme Court Justice William Rehnquist thinks these laws have more to do with politics than criminology. "Mandatory minimums," he has said, "are frequently the result of floor amendments to demonstrate emphatically that legislators want 'to get tough on crime.'"

Throughout the 1980s, lawmakers competed with one another to introduce ever-harsher penalties. States like California ratcheted up their anti-drug efforts, deploying helicopters in paramilitary crackdowns on marijuana growers. President Ronald Reagan doubled the FBI's budget, boosted spending on federal prisons, and expanded drug prosecutions—even though crime rates were falling. The crusading spirit was so contagious that even liberals like Walter Mondale, Reagan's opponent in the 1984 election, advocated using the armed forces to fight drugs.

The War on Drugs

The battle against drugs erupted into full-scale war when a new drug called crack began spreading in the inner cities, bringing with it a surge of violent crime—and an epidemic of fevered media coverage. "In the summer of '86, members of Congress were literally elbowing each other aside for TV time to talk about drugs," recalls Eric Sterling, who served then as counsel to the House Judiciary Committee. A new wave of laws boosting penalties still higher for drug offenders soon followed. Drugs were taking the place of the Cold War as an issue on which politicians could try to out-posture each other. "In the mid-1980s, there was general prosperity and the Soviets were not a threat," adds Zimring. "We were running out of enemies. Crack was the narcotic equivalent of the H-bomb scare."

A clear lesson had emerged: For politicians, crime pays: George [H.W.] Bush proved it in 1988, when he summoned the specter of paroled rapist Will Horton to haunt [Democratic challenger] Michael Dukakis out of the election. Bill Clinton topped him in 1992 by leaving the campaign trail to personally deny clemency to a mentally retarded man on death row in Arkansas.

Punishment had become a solidly bipartisan issue. In 1994, with crime on the decline for four years, Congress approved yet another major anti-crime package, raising drug penalties and providing billions of dollars for more prisons and police. In the early 1990s, the federal government and 23 states ratcheted up the mandatory-minimum concept another notch, by passing "three strikes" laws dictating prison sentences of 25 years to life for third felonies. These laws have undoubtedly taken some violent offenders out of circulation—but they have also handed out life sentences to thousands of people for petty crimes from possessing a stolen bicycle or stealing a spare tire.

"The prison boom has . . . exacted a tremendous social cost."

By now, federal surveys show there are more than 236,000 drug offenders in state prisons—more than 10 times the 1980 figure. The surge in the number of drug prisoners has leveled off in recent years, but prison populations continue to grow, thanks in large part to increases in sentencing. Now, "it's less about more people going in than about people staying longer," says Allen Beck, chief of correctional statistics at the federal Bureau of Justice Statistics.

Costs of Incarceration

Locking up so many inmates is not cheap. *Design-Build*, a construction trade magazine, estimates that 3,300 new prisons were built during the 1990s at a cost of nearly $27 billion, with another 268 in the pipeline valued at an additional $2.4 billion. And construction costs are only the beginning. In Los Angeles, the Twin Towers complex sat empty for over a year after it was completed because the county had run short of money to operate it.

Housing each prisoner costs taxpayers around $20,000 per year—money that often comes at the expense of other social programs. Between 1980 and 1996, prison spending shot up in every state, while spending on higher education declined in 19 states. In May [2001], Colorado lawmakers diverted $59 million earmarked for improving colleges and universities into paying for prison expansion.

The prison boom has also exacted a tremendous social cost. Blacks, Hispanics, and Native Americans are all incarcerated at rates far higher than that for whites. On any given day, nearly a third of all young black males are in prison, on probation, or on parole. Blacks are more likely than whites to be arrested, convicted, and given longer sentences for drug offenses—despite surveys showing that whites use drugs at the same rate as blacks do.

There are signs, however, that America may finally be sobering up from its two-decade incarceration binge. "Drug courts" that allow judges to order offenders into treatment rather than jail are gaining favor across the country. New York is looking at rewriting its harsh drug laws. Voters in many states have approved medical-marijuana initiatives in recent years. And many political leaders, including conservatives like [former] New Mexico governor Gary Johnson, are calling for a less-punitive approach to drugs. Perhaps partly as a result, in the past few years prison populations have declined slightly in 11 states.

> *"The media . . . have a vested interest in perpetuating the notion that crime is out of control."*

At the same time, a grassroots anti-prison movement is flowering across the country, from student campaigns to force campus caterer Sodexho-Marriott to divest their holdings in private prisons, to advocacy groups like Families Against Mandatory Minimums. "In the '80s all the prison activists were aging '60s people like me," says Ruthie Gilmore, a veteran organizer in California. "But now there are many more young people and families of prisoners, especially mothers, involved. It's still much smaller than, say, the '80s anti-apartheid movement, but it's going in that direction."

Perpetuating the Crime Myth

But while there are more critics of prisons today, there are also more interest groups with a financial stake in the incarceration complex—groups with a powerful incentive to ensure that the influx of inmates continues. Private, for-profit prison corporations are a multibillion dollar industry. Other companies reap hundreds of millions of dollars annually by providing health care, phones, food, and other services in correctional facilities. Many small towns and rural communities, their traditional industries in decline, lobby for new prisons in their areas. Such forces are working actively to increase the number of citizens being locked up. Private prison companies contribute to a policy group called the American Legislative Exchange Council that has helped draft tougher sentencing laws in dozens of states, and the California prison guards union doles out millions every election to tough-on-crime candidates.

The media, especially television, also have a vested interest in perpetuating the notion that crime is out of control. With new competition from cable networks and 24-hour news channels, TV news and programs about crime—dramatic, cheap to produce, and popular—have proliferated madly. According to the Center for Media and Public Affairs, crime coverage was the number-one topic on the nightly news over the past decade. From 1990 to 1998, homicide rates dropped by half nationwide, but homicide stories on the three major networks rose almost fourfold.

Such saturation coverage has a direct impact on public perceptions. In one 1997 survey, 80 percent of those polled said that news stories about violent crime increase their fear of being victimized. As a result, it has become "impossible to run an election campaign without advocating more jails, harsher punishment, more executions, all the things that have never worked to reduce crime but have always worked to get votes," concludes George Gerbner, former dean of University of Pennsylvania's Annenberg School of Communications and one of the nation's foremost experts on the media. "It's driven largely, although not exclusively, by television-cultivated insecurity."

While prison growth has slowed in the last couple of years, it's a long way from stopping. From mid-1999 to mid-2000, the number of people behind bars nationwide rose by 56,660. And the Bush administration has made clear that it is committed to continuing the push for more prisons. After all, as governor of Texas, George W. Bush oversaw a correctional system that locks up residents at a higher rate than any other state except Louisiana. The attorney general, John Ashcroft, and the drug czar, John Walters, are both renowned hard-liners. And in its very first budget proposal, the Bush team laid out an explicit priority: more money for federal prisons, to the tune of $1 billion.

The Threat of Incarceration Does Not Deter Criminal Behavior

by Stuart Henry

About the author: *Stuart Henry is a professor of interdisciplinary studies at Wayne State University in Detroit, Michigan.*

The issue of punishment is emotionally charged, misunderstood and nothing if not uncertain in its outcome. The central question is "Does Punishment Work?" The answer clearly depends on what is meant by "punishment" and what is meant by "work." Also important, is for whom is punishment effective, and by what mechanism? For example, are potential offenders likely to be affected by, even deterred by the existence of punishment? Are the kinds of behavior that are changeable through punishment the same as those which we classify as crime? In other words, are all behaviors equally able to be reduced or eliminated by the use of punishment? In addition, is the effective mechanism in the use of punishment its severity or the effectiveness/certainty of punishment as a consequence for the behavior? Finally, is prison an effective method of punishment for crime, or are other methods more effective in bringing about reductions in crime and changes in harmful behavior?

Assumptions About Punishment and Crime

The empirical question of the effectiveness of punishment is considerably clouded by the commonsense view of the efficacy of punishment. Most people believe punishment works because they use it in their everyday life, with their children, their co-workers and their pets, and, are themselves subject to it. Indeed, [according to the 2001 article "The Facts About Punishment" by Susan Friedman and Bobbi Brinker,]

> punishment is what most of us do . . . first. It is our teaching legacy passed down from generation to generation. We are virtually surrounded by punishing

Stuart Henry, "On the Effectiveness of Prison as Punishment," *Conference: Incarceration Nation: The Warehousing of America's Poor*, October 24, 2003, Ivy Tech State College, South Bend, Indiana. Reproduced by permission of the author.

strategies used to influence our behavior: From overdue library books to dogs without licenses; fines, penalties and reprimands whirl around us like leaves in a storm. For many of us, to give up punishment as our primary tool with which to influence negative behavior is to leave us empty handed.

Not surprisingly, the populist pro-punishment stance is reflected in public opinion surveys on the value of punishment, particularly extreme punishments like prison and the death penalty. According to punishment advocates like Morgan Reynolds of the Texas-based National Center for Policy Analysis [NCPA]:

> The answer is obvious to most Americans—yes, of course punishment reduces crime. Punishment converts criminal activity from a paying proposition to a nonpaying proposition, at least sometimes, and people respond accordingly. We all are aware of how similar incentives work in our lives, for example, choosing whether or not to drive faster than the law allows. . . . Incentives matter, including the risks we are willing to run. This is only a commonsense observation about how people choose to behave. . . . Public opinion strongly supports the increased use of prisons to give criminals their just deserts. The endorsement of punishment is relatively uniform across all groups. More than three-quarters of the public see punishment as the primary justification for sentencing. More than 70 percent believe that incapacitation is the only sure way to prevent future crimes, and more than three-quarters believe that the courts are too easy on criminals. Three-quarters favor the death penalty for murder.

Notice, however, that these beliefs are based on two conservative philosophies: (1) "incapacitation" i.e. that prison stops offenders incarcerated from offending while they are in prison, and (2) "just deserts" that those who commit crime deserve to be punished. The question of whether punishment is effective, is much more problematic, even though many, particularly economists who study crime, such as Isaac Ehrlich and Gary Becker, and criminological advocates from the political right, such as Charles Murray claim to have demonstrated evidence that it reduces crime by deterrence. So what do we know about the effectiveness of punishment, and in particular, what do we know about prison as an effective punishment? To answer this we need to first define punishment.

Defining Punishment and How It Works

What is punishment? Most psychologists define punishment as a process of presenting a consequence, delivered after a behavior, which serves to reduce the frequency or intensity with which the behavior occurs. The consequence, i.e. the punishment, can either be providing an undesirable stimulus or removing a desirable stimulus. In either case the idea is that punishment decreases the probability of the behavior occurring again.

There are two mechanisms that explain how punishment works to suppress unwanted behavior. The economic model is that of rational calculation: punishment is painful and therefore a cost which will be avoided; if the punishment is associated with the behavior, avoidance of pain is accomplished by avoidance of the behavior. The psychological model is that of learning through conditioned responses: repeated associations made between a behavior and aversive stimulus or removal of desired stimulus or positive reinforcer can, over time, lead to an "automatic" learned response to avoid the behavior.

> *"Punishment, especially in its severe form, has several negative effects."*

It is also important to appreciate that punishment can vary in intensity along a continuum from mild to severe [according to Friedman and Brinker in "The Facts About Punishment"]: "Punishment is not one single strategy but a collection of strategies that exist on a continuum from very mild to highly aversive approaches. Given our definition of punishment as a behavior-reducing technique, it is important to understand the nature of this continuum."

Punishment Effectiveness

The effectiveness of punishment relates to how far it is successful in suppressing the undesired behavior. Effectiveness depends upon practices that work in general, and those that work with specific populations; the effects are not necessarily the same.

Psychological research on punishment has shown that *mild* punishment can be effective in changing behavior, but the evidence is less clear about the effectiveness of severe punishment. Effectiveness of punishment is increased by:
1. Frequency of application
2. Immediacy of application
3. Punishment used in conjunction with positive reinforcement of pro-social behavior

However, punishment, especially in its severe form, has several negative effects:
1. Avoidance or escape
2. Alienation of those punished, to the point of inaction
3. Aggressiveness, both targeted and generalized, by those punished
4. Conditioning of the punishers through rewarding them for behavioral change
5. Reproducing punishment behavior in those punished

Crucial seems to be the relationship between effectiveness and severity. In criminal justice this translates into whether certainty of apprehension is more effective than the severity of punishment. Clearly if there was a severe punishment but no one got caught, the likely effect on behavior change because of the punishment would be low. Alternatively, having a high certainty of getting caught with no consequences is not likely to prove effective (although, because of the apprehension effect, it still has some ability to depress the occurrence of unwanted behavior). An optimization of a low to moderate punishment combined with a moderate to high certainty of apprehension seems to be the most effective combination. In criminal justice terms this translates to increased levels of policing. Evidence shows that increased levels of policing produce a substantial reduction in crime over time, and that this effect is enhanced when police efforts are targeted at certain problem areas. Indeed, even advocates of punishment, like Reynolds, concede this point:

> Scholars also ask which provides the greater deterrent, certainty or severity of punishment? One provocative study involving prisoners and college students came down firmly on the side of certainty. When tested, both groups responded in virtually identical terms. Prisoners could identify their financial self-interest in an experimental setting as well as students could. However, in their decision-making, prisoners were much more sensitive to changes in certainty than in severity of punishment. In terms of real-world application, the authors of the study speculate that long prison terms are likely to be more impressive to lawmakers than lawbreakers. . . . Supporting evidence for this viewpoint comes from a National Academy of Sciences panel, which claimed that a 50 percent increase in the probability of incarceration prevents about twice as much violent crime as a 50 percent increase in the average term of incarceration.

The Relationship Between Crime and Imprisonment

While research by Charles Murray and the NCPA has claimed that increasing the probability of severe sentences for crimes can reduce the incidence of crimes committed, there is little consensus among criminologists about this and general agreement that just increasing the severity of punishment for specific crimes does not reduce their occurrence. Murray, in his 1997 paper "Does Prison Work?" argues that the crime rate declines in relation to the sentence per crime and rises when the sentence per crime falls. He says that in the US the 10-year decline in the crime rate from the period 1990–2000, at 5% per year, resulted in one third less assaults, 50% less burglaries and 66% less robberies, and 75% less auto theft. This correlated with a substantially higher rate of imprisonment per population and a rising rate of imprisonment per recorded crime. He concludes that the crime reduction in the US is a direct result of the policy of imprisonment, which has both a deterrence effect and an incapacitation effect. Moreover, he believes that offenders should be incarcerated even when the crime rate is low, as prison sentences can stop rising crime and reverse the trend. Others have applied Murray's findings and drawn similar conclusions.

Critics charge that demonstrating a correlation is not establishing a cause; that rates are aggregate for the US and ignore important state differences; that crime rates have risen again after 2000 while the incapacitation and sentence/crime imprisonment population both remained high; and that the reliance on official crimes known to the police and use of index crime rather than all crime, make the analysis highly suspect. Others point to at least 14 explanations for the decline in the US crime rate during the period covered including: (1) a strong economy and low unemployment; (2) a decline in the nature of drug markets, especially a change in the crack-cocaine market; (3) a reduction in the number of young males in the population as the 1960s birth cohort matured; (4) increased law enforcement budgets under the Clinton presidency; (5) increased adoption of community policing strategies. Clearly whether crime was reduced as a result of higher prison sentences or other factors is an open question, although the combination of factors probably had a significant impact. However, we should be extremely cautious since the improved economy argument is potentially very significant, especially for the rational choice argument. Most research has consistently shown that unemployment is correlated with increased levels of crime. In particular, if the rational choice argument is believed, that during full employment potential offenders commit less recorded crime, then why is it not also likely that potential offenders among the formerly unemployed would, when employed, choose to commit their crime in the relatively unpoliced privacy of their workplace. Here they can engage in property offenses, with virtually no risk of prosecution and incarceration, rather than the relatively high risk/cost arenas of the street? Thus the rational choice model here would predict that there would be a reduction of officially recorded crime during high employment, not because of severe punishments, but because of a shift of crime reward opportunities from the risk-averse public arena to the risk-free workplace. In addition, the whole question of whether a prison is an effective punishment begs the question of whether prison as a punishment is perceived by potential offenders as a cost, and if so, to whom and for what kinds of behavior?

> *"Clearly whether crime was reduced as a result of higher prison sentences or other factors is an open question."*

Prison as an Effective Punishment?

There is no question that prison is seen as a severe punishment for most people. The critical question is whether it is an effective punishment for potential offenders. This depends on what motivates potential offenders. The deterrence argument is based on the arguments of economic rational choice theory and the classical assumption that offenders are self-interested, reasoning, rational cost-benefit calculators. However, much of the criminological literature has demonstrated that there are a variety of motivations that shape criminal activity ranging from biological predispositions, psychological personality traits, social learning, cognitive thinking, geographical location and the ecology of place, relative deprivation and the strain of capitalist society, political conflict and social and sub-cultural meaning. The result is that most criminologists reject the arguments of pure rationality contained in Ehrlich and Becker's utility and wealth maximization theories. Even those like G. Clarke and W. Cornish, who favor the rational choice argument, advocate the idea of "limited rationality." Indeed, as supporters of Murray's argument [according to Pete Saunders and Nicole Billante] are forced to concede: "The economic theory of crime that has developed out of Becker . . . recognizes that different individuals break the law for different reasons, that not all law breakers are rational utility maximizers, and that different offenders will weight the risks of benefits in different ways." So, who are the offenders who are supposedly influenced to reduce their commission of crime by deterrence through the severity of prison as a punishment? To answer this question we need to examine who are prisoners, and what are their crimes.

There are four key facts on prisoners and their crimes: (1) demographics, such as the gender, race and age of prisoners; (2) their level of education; (3) the nature of their offenses, and (4) their criminal history. [Bureau of Justice Statistics] data for 1997 shows . . . us that 67% of the state prison population are male, Black, Hispanic or other non-white and that 86.8% are aged between 18 and 44; in other words, young minority males. Moreover, the data also shows that this population is relatively illiterate compared with the US population as a whole, with 40% functional illiteracy rate compared with 21% among the population as a whole.

One might conclude that those incarcerated are less likely to be rational, cost-benefit calculators. Indeed, a look at incarcerated offenders criminal history supports exactly this point. Data [from the Open Society organization] shows that the national rearrest rate is 63%, although can be as high as 84% for juveniles but that 76% of the state prison population has a previous criminal history of prior convictions. The data for 1997 shows that almost half of those with prior convictions are for violent offenses. Importantly, 59% of recidivists have more than two previous convictions and 43% have more than 3 convictions.

Clearly, the threat of prison as punishment did not work for the majority of these offenders. This picture of the deterrence effect of prison as punishment is further undermined when examining the kinds of crimes that those in state prison have committed.

Of these offenses, only 22% are property crimes, the most likely to be deterrable; the rest are violent or drugs crimes, the least likely to be deterrable since they are typically motivated by irrational, expressive acts, or are the result of addiction or behavioral and personality problems. Indeed, only 10.7% of crimes are "burglaries" which are those most frequently cited as "deterrable" by prison as punishment advocates. In short, neither the majority of offenders nor the types of offenses committed by state convicted prisoners are of a kind that are the outcome

> *"Different individuals break the law for different reasons, . . . and . . . will weight the risks of benefits in different ways."*

of cost-benefit calculations that take account of the potential prison sentence, prior to the act.

Research over the past 10 years has consistently demonstrated that the most effective way to reduce offending, and particularly reoffending is through education, particularly literacy training and GED [general equivalency diploma].

An Arizona Department of Adult Probation Study showed that probationers who received literacy training had a 35% rearrest rate compared with a control group that had a 46% rearrest, and those who received a GED had a rearrest rate of 24%. Less dramatic but equally encouraging results were received from a [2003] Florida [Department of Corrections] study of 18,414 inmates released from prison in fiscal year 1996–97 followed up after 2 years, which found that "inmates who earn a GED are 8.7% less likely to recidivate than those who do not complete a program. . . . Inmates who receive a GED and improve their TABE [Tests of Adult Basic Education] score to 9th grade level or higher are 25.0% less likely to recidivate than those who receive a GED and have a TABE level of 8th grade or less." The Florida study also found that "academic program impacts are found even among offender groups that normally have higher recidivism, for example, males, younger males, black offenders and prior recidivists." Importantly, a [2001] New York State study found that "young inmates who earned a GED while incarcerated returned to custody at a rate of 40% compared with 54% of inmates under 21 released with no degree." Most dramatic, however, is the data on those in prison: Inmates with at least two years college education have a 10% rearrest rate, compared to the national rearrest rate of 62%. A Texas study is most revealing showing that the overall recidivism rate for degree holders in the Texas Department of Corrections between 1990 and 1991 was 15% compared to 60% for the national rate and a two year follow-up study showed that those with associates degrees had a recidivism rate of 13.7%, those with bachelor's degrees, 5.6%, and those with master's degrees zero.

> *"Only 10.7% of crimes are 'burglaries' which are . . . frequently cited as 'deterrable' by prison as punishment advocates."*

Expand Solutions Beyond Imprisonment

So, if the evidence is clear that prison as punishment is ineffective in deterring offenders, but education makes a substantial difference to recidivism, why do we continue to use prison as punishment? Moreover, why did we stop using education, particularly college-level education, for prisoners? The analogy of criminal justice and social policy as a "toolbox" comes to mind. We have many "tools" each refined for serving different functions. Just as a screwdriver, hammer, saw, wrench serves different functions to solve technical problems, so various policy options are available to deal with crime problems, whether this is biologically based treatment, psychologically based therapy, sociologically based education and training, and economically based punishment. However, it seems that policy makers peering into the justice toolbox only see one tool, the hammer of punishment, and they try to use it to fix everything. Imagine what would happen if your plumber showed up to fix a leak and all he had was a hammer. Imagine if you took your car to be serviced and all they had was a hammer! Why, given the bio-social, psycho-political complexity of human beings do we restrict our policy to this one-dimensional approach. It makes no sense. Indeed, we seem to have a better appreciation for how to bring behavioral change in parrots than in people. As noted parrot experts [Friedman and Brinker in "The Facts About Punishment"] say:

> There will always be many unknowns about behavior; there will always be important variables that are out of our control. Behavior is just too complex for simplistic cookbook approaches to mentoring our birds. . . . Each situation is unique and requires careful analysis and informed consideration. Facilitating well-adjusted, independent, confident companion parrots through the use of positive teaching techniques is more than just a commitment to learning new strategies; it is also a commitment to changing our legacy. The time for such change is now.

So what *are* the policy implications of the prison-as-punishment does not deter crime conclusion? First, we need to consider ceasing to use prison as punishment. Incapacitating the most seriously harmful offenders is a different argument. Second, we should draw on the research of what we know works to prevent recidivism, especially literacy programs, skills training and GED, as well as educating prisoners to associate's degree level in higher education and restore financial support for these successful practices. Third, we should train corrections officers to be *corrections* officers rather than guards, and if that means training them to be effective and qualified teachers, then this will be money well spent. Fourth, we should invest the money spent on incarceration on ensuring that the illiteracy rate among the nation's population is reduced dramatically. Doing so will ensure that our general population is equipped to make the very kind of rational choice decisions that will enable them to make better choices in the first place. Finally, we should abandon the discourse of punishment as our response to unwanted behavior. It doesn't work for parrots and it doesn't work for people.

The Expanding Prison System Is Socially Unjust

by Marc Mauer

About the author: *Marc Mauer is the author of* Race to Incarcerate *and assistant director of the Sentencing Project, a nonprofit organization that promotes criminal justice reform.*

In the mid-1980s, the United States was wracked by a profound health crisis that was both unique and frightening. As the nation began to learn of the rapid spread of the HIV virus, major federal resources and public attention were focused on attempting to understand the source of the virus and finding a way to respond to it. Fifteen years later, the virus has taken a tremendous toll in human lives and suffering, but major progress has been made as well. AIDS education and prevention curricula are now commonplace in a vast array of school and community settings, and the rapid development of new drug therapies has served to enable many with the disease to continue to lead productive lives.

Coincident with the rapid spread of AIDS in the mid-1980s was another epidemic that also brought great tragedy and suffering. This epidemic was one of violence associated with the introduction and spread of crack cocaine, initially in urban areas and then in other communities. As teenagers and others in many neighborhoods armed themselves with lethal weapons to protect their drug "turf," murder rates spiked sharply in the second half of the 1980s, particularly among African American males.

Policymakers' reaction to crack cocaine and violence was swift and certain. A host of harsh sentencing laws was adopted, the most notorious being the federal provisions providing for a mandatory five years of incarceration for possession of five grams of crack—the weight of two pennies. Along with this came a veritable orgy of new prison construction that has sent the nation's prison population soaring from 500,000 in 1980 to nearly two million [in 2002]. This building frenzy served to accelerate the prison expansion that had begun in the 1970s, which has led to the United States now having attained the dubious distinction of maintaining the world's highest rate of incarceration, recently surpassing Russia for this honor.

Treating Two Epidemics

The two epidemics of the 1980s offer a useful opportunity to contrast the development of public policy. Imagine for the moment that in response to the AIDS epidemic, national leaders had instead proclaimed a policy of massive hospital construction to cope with the sick and dying population. Ever-larger institutions would have been built through infusions of federal and state funds, even as the death toll continued to mount. No budget increases would have been sought for federal research on the disease or for investigating personal lifestyle changes to reduce the chances of contagion.

The notion of confronting a health crisis by building hospitals is ludicrous, of course, but in our national imagination the idea of building prisons to confront a crime problem has become the policy of choice. How, then, did we come to view these two crises in such different terms?

First, to be sure, the national response to AIDS was far from an entirely compassionate one from the beginning. As AIDS was initially perceived as a "gay disease," some Americans viewed it as a deserved punishment for "immoral" behavior. And political leaders in many cases acted only reluctantly after massive mobilizations by the gay community and public-health advocates. But in no instance did the notion of hospital construction as a "solution" ever enter anyone's mind.

Why we view disease and crime in such strikingly different terms is complex, but several factors can help us understand the roots of this dichotomy. First, many Americans quickly realized that a sexually transmitted disease was a threat not just to others but also to themselves and their loved ones. As such, "blaming the victim" was hardly an approach to bring comfort in most homes. And as more "celebrity" victims emerged, the public face of the disease changed, and a more compassionate and public health-oriented response emerged.

In examining the crime problem, though, the public perception of the "criminal" has become predominant in determining the direction of policy. Just as various waves of European immigrants were viewed as the source of the crime problem in the early years of the twentieth century, so too have African Americans now become the public image of the "criminal." As

> *"The United States [has] attained the dubious distinction of maintaining the world's highest rate of incarceration."*

this perception has become more pervasive, the policy response that has developed has been one that emphasizes punishment and incarceration over an approach that engages the nation in a search for causes and cures.

Just to be clear at this point—suggesting that we examine comprehensive approaches to problems such as crime does not absolve individuals of responsibility for their actions or suggest that crime, and particularly violent crime, is not a serious problem for the nation. But if we are to develop policy options that make the most effective use of scarce resources while also building on the strengths of communities, then we are obligated to consider a variety of frameworks for approaching such problems.

Prevailing crime policies should prove troubling to all Americans. First, we maintain the odd position of being the wealthiest society in human history while also locking up more of our citizens than any nation has ever done before. Second, the racial dynamics of this policy are profound: at current rates of imprisonment 29 percent of black males born today can expect to go to prison at some point in their lives, as well as 16 percent of Latino males (and 4 percent of white males). Surely these are not trends that should be welcomed, regardless of one's beliefs about the causes of such developments. . . .

> *"At current rates of imprisonment 29 percent of black males . . . can expect to go to prison."*

Effects of Prevailing Policy on Society

While examining the prison/crime relationship is important, it risks obscuring a deeper analysis of the effects of imprisonment on society. In times past, these issues were rarely explored. The experience of imprisonment clearly affected the individual inmate and his or her family, but the impact was not one that necessarily expanded beyond the family. But at the level of incarceration that we have reached today—an era of "mass imprisonment," as described by some—an analysis of the impact of imprisonment must of necessity go beyond the individual prisoner and explore how our policies affect society broadly.

Not surprisingly, this impact is felt most dramatically in the African American community, given the astonishing rates of incarceration that currently prevail. Among adult black males, one in twenty-one is in prison or jail on any given day. In the twenty-five to thirty-four age group, the figure reaches one in eight. Comparable figures for black women are lower overall, but have been rising at dramatic rates and outpace the incarceration of white women by a ratio of six to one.

While about half of black prisoners are incarcerated for violent offenses (as is true for all racial/ethnic groups), the explosion of drug sentences has affected African Americans profoundly. African Americans currently constitute 58 percent of all drug offenders in state prisons (and Latinos an additional 21 percent), while government surveys document that blacks represent only 13 percent of monthly drug users. The reasons for the disparity between drug use and incarceration are complex but in large part reflect two distinct approaches to the problem of substance abuse—a public-health approach emphasizing treatment in middle-income communities and a law-enforcement approach using incarceration in inner-city neighborhoods.

High rates of imprisonment in black communities have a direct effect on family structure. One of every fourteen black children today has a parent who is locked up; over the course of a year, or especially over the duration of childhood, the figures are considerably higher. How does this affect the fourth grader who is "acting out" in class, trying to cope both with the absence of a parent and with the stigma brought upon the family?

The economic effects on communities become profound as well. A stint in prison is hardly an impressive component of one's resume, and ex-offenders returning to the community find themselves competing for even low-wage, low-skill employment. In broad terms, this then translates into less economic and social capital in low-income communities, and thus the beginnings of a vicious cycle that creates the underpinnings of neighborhoods where crime may flourish.

The punitive approach to social policy represented by mass incarceration has expanded to related areas of policy, often in ways that are dramatically at odds with effective crime-policy approaches. One such step was the 1994 decision by Congress to prohibit inmates from receiving Pell grants to pursue college education while in prison. Before that, the relative handful of prisoners with a high school degree and motivation to attend college could take advantage of college courses offered at prisons in many states by local institutions of higher education. Nationally, less than one percent of all Pell grant money went to support such programs. But in an act that can only be characterized as meanspirited, Congress cut this funding source. As a result, prison college programs in many states have dried up. The plain fact is that research has consistently shown that education is associated with reduced recidivism. So while the policy is "anticriminal," it is certainly not "anticrime."

> *"High rates of imprisonment in black communities have a direct effect on family structure."*

Two years later Congress continued the excesses of the "war on drugs" as part of the passage of welfare-reform legislation. A little-noticed provision of the 1996 bill stipulated that anyone convicted of a felony drug offense would henceforth be barred from receiving welfare benefits for life, unless individual states opted out of the provision. Thus, under the logic of this policy, a three-time armed robber who is released from prison is eligible for welfare benefits but not a struggling single mother who engages in a one-time drug sale. Here, too, the effect of national policy will be to make it even more difficult for the largely female prisoners returning home after serving drug sentences who might need temporary welfare assistance to make the transition back to family life. It is unlikely that such a policy will have any deterrent effect on drug selling, but it is quite certain that it will have deleterious effects on many poor women and their children.

The movement toward mass incarceration is also affecting our democratic processes in ways that are increasingly profound. One such impact comes through policies that strip away the voting rights of convicted felons. Each state has its own policies in this regard, but in forty-eight states prisoners are not eligible to vote; in thirty-two states felons on probation and/or parole are excluded from voting; in thirteen states ex-felons who have completed their sentences can still be barred from voting, in most cases for life. Thus, for example, an eighteen-year-old in Virginia who is convicted of selling drugs to an undercover agent is forever barred from the ballot box, even if he lives a crime-free life afterward. The only means of gaining one's rights back are through a gubernatorial pardon, a time-consuming and cumbersome process in many states.

> *"There are far more effective, and socially less destructive, ways to affect crime [than imprisonment]."*

While these laws have existed in some states since the founding of the nation, the scale of imprisonment today results in disenfranchisement rates that are far from trivial. Nationally, about four million Americans—two percent of the voting-age population—are currently barred from voting as the result of a current or prior felony conviction. Among African American males, the rates are much higher, an estimated 1.4 million citizens, or 13 percent of that population. In the historic 2000 presidential election, the exclusion of at least 200,000 ex-felons in Florida was clearly of such magnitude as to have potentially altered the course of the election.

The scope of these collateral effects of incarceration might be viewed by some as merely unfortunate by-products of an otherwise necessary approach to crime. But we have seen in recent years that there are far more effective, and socially less destructive, ways to affect crime. In Boston, a collaborative effort between criminal-justice agencies and community groups has resulted in an impressive reduction in youth violence. In states across the country, drug courts are now diverting addicted offenders into court-supervised treatment rather than prison. And many communities are engaged in restorative justice programs that bring together victims and offenders to engage in a process of fashioning appropriate ways for offenders to make victims whole again while also addressing the underlying causes of crime.

No single program or approach in itself offers a panacea for crime. But what is becoming increasingly clear is that the American mania for incarceration is having a broad set of consequences for the health of our society. To acknowledge this is not to suggest that crime is not a legitimate concern for all Americans but, rather, to encourage a reassessment of how we address this problem in a way that draws on the strengths of families and communities rather than increasing their fragility.

Building More Prisons Is Not Cost-Effective

by Cait Murphy

About the author: *Cait Murphy is senior editor at the business and finance magazine* Fortune.

America is an exceptional country. Compared with citizens of other nations, Americans tend to be more religious and more entrepreneurial. We send more people to university, have more millionaires, and enjoy more living space. We are the world leaders in obesity and Nobel Prizes.

Prison Economics

And we send people to prison at a rate that is almost unheard of. Right now, almost two million Americans are either in prison (after conviction) or jail (waiting for trial). Of every 100,000 Americans, 481 are in prison. By comparison, the incarceration rate for Britain is 125 per 100,000, for Canada 129, and for Japan 40. Only Russia, at 685, is quicker to lock 'em up.

America was not always so exceptional in this regard. For the 50 years prior to 1975, the U.S. incarceration rate averaged about 110, right around rich-world norms. But then, in the 1970s, the great prison buildup began. This was a bipartisan movement. Democrats like Jerry Brown of California and Ann Richards of Texas, for example, presided over prison population booms, as did Republican governors like John Ashcroft of Missouri and Michael Castle of Delaware. Bill Clinton worried in public about rising prison populations but signed legislation, much of it Republican sponsored, that kept the figures rising. No surprise, then, that spending on incarceration has ballooned from less than $7 billion in 1980 to about $45 billion today.

Just because the U.S. is different doesn't mean it is wrong. But prison is a serious matter in a way that, say, America's inexplicable affection for tractor pulls is not. Accordingly, a number of people—social scientists, prison professionals, even a few politicians—have begun to examine how and why the U.S. sends people to prison. What they are finding, in broad terms, is that there is a substantial minority of prisoners for whom incarceration is inappropriate—and much too expensive.

Who deserves to be imprisoned is, of course, partly a question of moral values. Prison keeps criminals off the streets; it punishes transgressors and deters people from committing crimes. But it is also a question of economic values. Everyone agrees that caging, say [serial killer] John Wayne Gacy is worth whatever it costs, but that locking up a granny caught shoplifting makes no sense. The question to consider, then, is not "Does prison work?" but "When does prison work?" Economics can help draw the line.

Understanding Prison Growth

On one level, it makes sense that America imprisons more people than its peers. The U.S. has historically been more violent than Europe, Japan, or Canada in particular, our homicide rate is well above world norms—and the public wants violent people punished while freeing society from their presence. "We are a culture that believes change is possible, that human beings can be saved," says Francis Cullen of the University of Cincinnati, who specializes in public attitudes toward crime and rehabilitation. "The dividing line is violence. That's where people start becoming unwilling to take risks.". . .

Fundamentally, America's prison population grew because people got sick of feeling scared and elected politicians who promised to deliver freedom from that fear. Moreover, it could be argued that America had some catching up to do: From the early 1960s to the early 1970s, the violent-crime rate rose sharply while the incarceration rate actually fell. Those trends probably helped spawn the "tough on crime" mentality that has reigned since. In the 1980s lawmakers delivered mandatory minimums—statutory requirements for harsh sentences for certain offenses, mostly gun- and drug-related. In the 1990s came "three-strikes" laws, designed to target repeat felons; truth-in-sentencing legislation; and the abolition of parole in many states.

All those policies filled prisons, but not necessarily with the hardened thugs people thought they were putting away. Though there are now 400,000 more violent offenders behind bars than there were in 1980, the proportion of violent offenders in the prison population has actually fallen. According to the Bureau of Justice Statistics [BJS], the percentage of violent offenders in state prisons has dropped from almost 60% in 1980 to 48% at the end of

> *"There is a substantial minority of prisoners for whom incarceration is inappropriate—and much too expensive."*

1999; 21% were in prison in 1999 for property crimes, 21% for drug crimes, and the rest for public-order offenses, such as immigration, vice, or weapons violations. In the federal system, home to about 145,000 offenders, 58% are in for drug offenses (compared with 25% in 1980) and only 12% for violent crimes—down from 17% in 1990. Of the six crimes that account for the great majority of prisoners (murder, robbery, aggravated assault, burglary, drugs, and sexual assault), drug offenders made up 45% of the growth from 1980 to 1996, figures Allen Beck of the BJS. Every year from 1990 through 1997, more people were sentenced to prison for drug offenses than for violent crimes.

More Prisons, Less Crime?

Because imprisonment went up in the 1990s and crime went down, you might conclude that locking up so many criminals bought us less crime. Up to a point that's true. Steven Levitt, a professor of economics at the University of Chicago, has cleverly provided an empirical foundation to prove the link between incarceration and crime reduction. In 1996 he studied what happened after the courts ordered 12 states to reduce overcrowding in their prison systems. By looking at how the states responded, either by releasing convicts or by building new prisons, he estimated that the effect of imprisoning one additional lawbreaker for a year was to prevent two fewer violent crimes and about a dozen fewer property crimes. The social costs of these crimes Levitt estimated at $53,900 (a figure derived from published estimates commonly used by social scientists). That's well above the $25,000 or so it costs to keep a prisoner behind bars for a year.

> *"There [are] ways to deliver just as much public safety for less money."*

But that doesn't prove that every prison cell built in America's 25-year construction spree was worth it. There could be ways to deliver just as much public safety for less money. Take Canada. Like the U.S., Canada saw a sharp decline in violent crime in the 1990s—but while America's prison population almost doubled, Canada's rose only slightly. Or take next-door neighbors New Hampshire and Maine. In the first half of the 1990s, both saw similar declines in crime, but New Hampshire sharply increased the number of people it imprisoned, while Maine did not. Ditto for Kansas and Missouri; the latter built lots more new prisons, but the crime rates in the two states remained similar. In short, building prisons is not the only way to fight crime—and often not a cost-effective way to do so.

In economic terms, this is because not every prison cell delivers equal returns, in terms of havoc unwreaked. As more and more people are imprisoned, the nastiness of the inmate population diminishes, so the crime control delivered per convict drops. Consider the research of John DiIulio, the new director of President [George W.] Bush's office of faith-based programs; Bert Useem, director of the Institute for Social Research at the University of New Mexico; and Anne Morrison Piehl, a professor of public policy at Harvard's Kennedy School of Government. In 1999 the trio surveyed male inmates in Arizona, New Mexico, and New York about their criminal pasts. Then they multiplied each crime by its social cost, using National Institute of Justice numbers. (The cost of a rape, for example, is estimated at $98,327; of a burglary, $1,271.)

Ranking the Costs of Crime

They found that the social cost of the crimes committed by the median inmate in New York—that is, one whose crimes rank 50 on a scale of 100 in terms of seriousness—was $31,866; in New Mexico, $26,486; and in Arizona, $25,472. That's slightly more than the $25,000 cost of incarceration. For the 40th percentile, though, that figure dropped to less than $14,000 in all three states, and for the 20th, less than $7,000. At

> *"It costs about $23 million to jail 94 people for a year."*

the 80th percentile, the monetary value of crime caused was almost $240,000 for New York and $163,311 for New Mexico—marking the perpetrator as the type of person for whom prison is clearly an appropriate solution.

The major dividing line between cost-effective and non-cost-effective incarceration? That turns out to be fairly easy to figure. As a general rule, those who were imprisoned for property or violent crimes caused damage to society that cost more than their incarceration; those convicted solely of drug offenses did not.

Drug dealing is not harmless, of course. Having an open-air crack market on the corner kills commerce and devastates neighborhoods. But the authors became convinced that the incarceration of so many drug-only offenders—28% in New York and 18% in Arizona—made no economic sense, because one drug seller sent to prison just created a job opening for another seller. Consider the example of a Milwaukee street corner. In 1996 a Wisconsin task force noted that although the police had made 94 drug-related arrests in three months at the corner of 9th and Concordia, most of them leading to prison sentences, the drug market continued and public safety did not improve. And the price was substantial: It costs about $23 million to jail 94 people for a year.

In short, the authors found that for drug offenders, "the crime averted by incarceration is low," says Piehl. "We need to come up with sanctions that are graduated so that our only options are not nothing, or prison, or probation." What made that conclusion particularly noteworthy was that Piehl and DiIulio had argued for years in favor of more prisons. But by [2000] DiIulio, who is no one's idea of a bleedingheart liberal, was writing an article for the editorial page of the *Wall Street Journal* titled "Two Million Prisoners Is Enough."

Less Costly Alternatives

Are there better, less costly alternatives to prison for drug offenders? Lisa Roberson offers one answer to that question. She is a resident at the Phoenix Career Academy in Brooklyn, N.Y., which offers residents—many of them repeat offenders who would otherwise be in prison-intensive drug treatment, vocational training, and after-care assistance. Roberson, 31, who started selling drugs at 17 and using them at 21, spent four years at Clinton State in New Jersey for selling drugs to an undercover cop. "All I did there is learn how to jail," she says. When she was arrested again in 2000, the court gave her a choice: prison or two years at Phoenix.

This is no country club. Residents sleep ten to a room. Just about every minute of their day, starting with a 6 A.M. wake-up call, is plotted for them. If Roberson makes it through the program—and about 60% do—she will be drug-free and will have completed training as a drug counselor. Phoenix will help her find a job, an apartment, and child care for her 4-year-old son. Yes, Roberson may regress—of those who complete the course, about a third eventually go back to drugs—but clearly she has a much better shot at establishing a real life than if she had spent several more years "learning how to jail." The cost of her treatment, funded mostly by state and local governments: $17,000 to $18,000 a year.

Many successful drug-treatment programs are run out of prisons too—such as Amity Righturn, a program in a medium-security facility in San Diego that provides more than a year of assessment and counseling, plus further treatment after the inmates have left prison. A 1999 study found that three years after release, 27% of inmates who completed all three parts of the program had returned to prison; among those who got no treatment, 75% did.

On the subject of drug treatment, cost-benefit analysis has something to say: It works. Numerous studies have concluded that well-run drug-treatment programs, particularly long-term residential ones with follow-up care, can pay for themselves just by reducing crime. Add in the value of incarceration avoided and taxes paid by the freed, and it adds up.

> *"For every dollar spent on basic adult education in prison, there was $1.71 in reduced crime."*

Given this context, it's little short of tragic that drug-treatment programs in prison are not keeping pace with the need for them. In 1991 about a third of the inmates who reported drug use in the month prior to their arrest were getting treatment; by 1999 that was down to less than 15%, according to the Department of Justice, and much of that was of the nonintensive variety that has little longterm effect. Treatment is no panacea: Lots of people will drop out or go back to their bad habits. The point is simply that treatment works often enough for the benefits to outweigh the costs—the exact opposite of the economics of prison for drug offenders.

Educational Programs Save Money

What about other prison programs? Social scientists have applied cost-benefit analysis to those too. They have found that busy inmates—those given the chance to learn to read, to finish high school, to learn basic job skills—are significantly less likely than idle ones to return to prison. In Maryland, for example, a follow-up analysis published in October [2002] of 1,000 former inmates found a 19% lower recidivism rate for those who had taken education programs in prison than for those who hadn't. Extrapolating that 19% figure for the state as a whole suggests that Maryland could save $23.2 million a year in reduced incarceration—double what it spends on prison education programs.

More evidence that educational programs save money: In 1999 analysts from the state of Washington surveyed studies dating back to the mid-1970s on what works and what fails in reducing crime. The researchers concluded that for every dollar spent on basic adult education in prison, there was $1.71 in reduced crime; for every dollar on vocational education, $3.23.

If you think such data have prompted more educational programs in prisons, think again. Congress passed "get tough" legislation in the 1990s that eliminated Pell grants to prisoners for college courses; it also reduced the requirements for basic and vocational education for prisoners. Many states have therefore taken the opportunity to cut back. Prisoners have a limited constituency, after all, and nixing programs for them is a politically painless way to cut budgets. Ironically, surveys show that the public strongly supports prisoner-rehabilitation programs. So do many who run the prisons. Tommy Douberley, warden of Florida's Moore Haven Correctional Facility, is convinced that no-frills prisons are a mistake. "These people are going to be returned to society," he says. "We need to make some provision for them that when they get out they are better than when they went in." Politicians, however, seem to have interpreted the public's clear desire for greater safety as a mandate for more and harsher prisons. And they are not the same thing at all.

There are signs that America is beginning to recognize the limits of prison. Drug offenders are less likely to be sentenced to prison today than they were in 1992 (though still more than three times as likely as in 1980), in part because of the emergence of drug courts in many states, which force defendants into treatment on pain of prison. But past policies continue to exert expansionary pressure. From June 1999 to June 2000, the last 12-month period for which figures are available, the incarcerated population rose 3%. Though the smallest rise in decades, that still meant that 31,000 more Americans were behind bars. To house them means building a prison every ten days or so—an expensive hobby, considering that a medium-security facility for 1,000 inmates can cost $50 million.

Make no mistake: A large proportion of inmates thoroughly deserve to be exactly where they are. Incarceration is an effective way to isolate really awful people. But too many prisons stuffed with nonviolent, idle inmates is simply wasteful, of both people and money. We would do better to learn from several states that have lowered the crime rate without substantially raising prison populations—as New York did at least in part by aggressively funneling drug offenders into treatment, for example. Instead of being exceptional for its willingness to jail its citizens, the goal for America should be to become exceptional in the application of wisdom to its criminal population. At the moment, it is not even close.

Chapter 2

How Should Inmates Be Treated?

Chapter Preface

Hundreds of thousands of U.S. criminals have been incarcerated since the mid-1970s, largely in response to public frustration with crime. Some tough-on-crime observers contend, however, that prison life is more of a vacation than a term of punishment. They cite inmate access to weight-training equipment, cable television, free health care, and hours of leisure at taxpayer expense as sending the wrong message to would-be criminals and crime victims. Explains journalist Dana Tofig, "Much of the public is fed up with crime, and pictures of basketball hoops and fully stocked libraries in prison only make them more disgusted." Indeed, debates about how inmates should be treated have grown more vociferous in recent years.

In response, politicians have shown a willingness to approve measures to make prisons more punitive. Senator John Ensign of Nevada has introduced legislation that would make prisoner participation in work programs mandatory and would curtail the perks granted to inmates. In Maricopa County, Arizona, inmates sleep outdoors in tents and are denied television and exercise equipment. More extreme, California, Texas, and Wisconsin have constructed supermaximum security prisons to isolate intractable, violent inmates who threaten the safety of prison staff and other inmates. In California's Pelican Bay State Prison, which opened in 1989, the majority of inmates are kept in windowless solitary confinement for nearly twenty-four hours a day. The only reprieve from cell confinement is a daily, ninety-minute exercise period within an enclosed concrete corridor. Perks like televisions and radios are granted only after an inmate demonstrates good behavior, and phone calls are forbidden. Visitors are allowed, but visitation must be conducted by phone through a sheet of plexiglass.

However, critics have expressed fears that tougher prisons may be turning violent offenders into angrier, less stable individuals. Argues Markku Salminen, the director general of prisons in Finland, "Brutal prisons make brutal prisoners. . . . The American system has made the American criminal very hard." Joe McGrath, warden of the Pelican Bay supermax prison, questions whether funneling inmates into increasingly punitive environments is the right approach to inmate violence. Says McGrath, "Violence is so great . . . in our prisons. . . . I'm the end of the road. Some prisoners get in trouble, oh, send them to Pelican Bay. Well, what do I do with them?" McGrath implies that ignoring the underlying causes of prisoner violence is a dead end that serves neither prisoners nor the interests of public safety.

Whether harsher prisons exacerbate inmate violence is just one of the subjects examined in the following chapter. To be sure, the treatment of inmates in America's prisons is hotly debated by prison officials, human rights organizations, and politicians from every state.

Incarceration Should Be Punitive

by John Ensign

About the author: *John Ensign is a U.S. senator from the state of Nevada.*

Editor's Note: The following viewpoint was originally delivered as a statement before the U.S. Senate on March 20, 2003, in support of the Mandatory Prisoner Work and Drug Testing Act. As of spring 2004, the act remains under evaluation by a Senate committee.

I rise today to introduce the Mandatory Prisoner Work and Drug Testing Act of 2003. This legislation is the continuation of work I did while in the House of Representatives to rein in the undeserved privileges that are currently given to federal prisoners.

Discipline, Rehabilitation, and Restitution

Today's criminal justice system is failing, partly because of what happens (or more specifically, doesn't happen) once convicted criminals arrive in prison. What prisoners are doing is watching cable television, getting high on drugs, lifting weights, and learning to be better criminals. What they are not doing is working and paying back their victims. That's not justice.

The purpose of the Mandatory Prisoner Work and Drug Testing Act is to help establish a federal prison system that provides discipline and rehabilitation for our nation's prisoners and requires that they make restitution to their victims.

First, this legislation requires that all federal prison inmates have a 50-hour work week. Job training, educational and life skills preparation study will also be mandated under this provision. Current federal law does not mandate a minimum work week for the 100,000 inmates in the federal prison system. Sadly, the average workday for a prisoner in the United States is 6.8 hours. This is absolutely unacceptable. American taxpayers should not have to work full-time to provide rest and relaxation for our nation's prisoners.

Jonh Ensign, statement before the U.S. Senate, Washington, DC, March 20, 2003.

Federal prisoners would be paid for the work they do, but their pay would be divided and dispersed in the following manner: 25 percent would offset the cost of prisoner incarceration, 25 percent would go to victim restitution, 25 percent would be made available to the inmate for necessary costs of incarceration, 10 percent would be placed in a non-interest bearing account to be paid to the inmate upon release, and the remaining 15 percent would go to states and local jurisdictions that operate correctional facilities which have similar programs.

> *"There is no reason for inmates to be given the same, or better, privileges than law-abiding citizens have."*

Second, this legislation requires the Bureau of Prisons to establish a zero-tolerance policy for the use or possession of illegal contraband. A drug-free environment is essential to any hopes of rehabilitation for our federal prison inmates. Under these provisions, inmates would be subject to random searches and inspections for drugs not less than 12 times each year. Federal prisons would be required to offer residential drug treatment for all inmates. And finally, any employee hired to work in a federal prison would undergo a mandatory drug test, and all employees would be subject to random testing at least twice each year.

I understand that many state and local prisons would also be interested in starting programs to get a drug-free prison, and for that reason have included a new grant program. Any state or unit of local government may apply for grants if they meet the same drug-testing requirements that are mandated for federal prisons under this legislation.

Hard Labor in Boot Camps

Third, the Mandatory Prisoner Work and Drug Treatment Act includes a requirement that all inmates in the federal prison system participate in a boot camp for not less than four weeks. This boot camp program would include strict discipline, physical training, and hard labor to deter crime and promote successful integration or reintegration of the offender into the prison community. Those prisoners that choose not to participate or are physically unable to participate are required to be confined to their cells for not less than 23 hours per day during the duration that they would otherwise be spending in this program and be allowed only those privileges that are granted under federal law.

These boot camps work. In fact, the Federal Bureau of Prisons already supports two such programs, one for men and one for women. These programs place inmates in highly structured, spartan environments where they undergo physical training and labor-intensive work assignments, coupled with education and vocational training, substance abuse treatment, and life skills programs. They focus on promoting positive changes in inmates' behavior, including responsible decision-making, self-direction and positive self-image. In fact, boot camps have worked so well that over 30 states now have them in place.

Finally, this legislation will further restrict inmates' activities and possessions. Under this legislation inmates would not be allowed to possess or smoke tobacco, view or read pornographic or sexually explicit material, or view cable television that is not educational in nature. Inmates would not be allowed to possess microwave ovens, hot plates, toaster ovens, televisions, or VCRs. They would not be allowed to listen to music that contains lyrics that are violent, vulgar, sexually explicit, glamorize gang membership or activities, demean women, or disrespect law enforcement. We have to remember that these individuals are in federal prison to be punished for a crime they committed. There is no reason for inmates to be given the same, or better, privileges than law-abiding citizens have. No one can tell me that an inmate has to have cable television when many law-abiding, taxpaying families cannot afford such a perk. . . .

We need to work to ensure that our nation's criminals understand the gravity of the crimes they committed. I understand that many of our nation's jails and prisons use activities like weight lifting as rewards for their inmates. My legislation does not restrict that kind of activity. This legislation simply states that it is no longer acceptable for our nation's inmates to leisurely go about their day instead of working to pay for the crimes they committed. It is time that our government send a clear message to the victims of these crimes that these criminals will pay, and that restitution, to the maximum extent possible, will be made.

Quite simply, we need to stop the revolving doors of our prison system. A study released in June 2002, by the U.S. Department of Justice found that among nearly 300,000 prisoners released in 15 states in 1994, 67.5 percent were rearrested within three years. It is my hope that if federal prisoners were required to work and given drug treatment, instead of perks like cable television and weight training time, these individuals would be deterred from committing another crime and returning to prison.

Harsher Prisons Exacerbate Criminal Behavior

by Kenneth L. McGinnis

About the author: *Kenneth L. McGinnis served as director of the Michigan Department of Corrections from 1991 to 1998.*

Over the last two decades, America has witnessed an ongoing campaign that promised to eradicate crime through policies promising maximum punishment and incapacitation. The results of this campaign are well known. The prison and jail populations of the United States have increased from approximately 500,000 to nearly 2 million persons, with an additional 3.8 million individuals on probation and parole. Even more staggering is the fact that 1 out of every 36 Americans is under the control of the criminal justice system.

Costly Incapacitation

While the debate over the effectiveness of this campaign of incapacitation to reduce crime and, more important, to reduce the fear of crime, rages throughout America, one thing is clear: The economic costs of imprisonment are enormous. In state after state, the desire to expand prison capacities has become embroiled in the reality that funding for education, social service programs, mental health services, and infrastructure improvements will have to be deferred or reduced to accommodate the growing corrections budgets. In Michigan, budgets for correctional programs grew from less than $300 million in 1980 to over $1.4 billion in 1998. One in every six dollars of state general revenue expenditures now goes to support prison, probation, and parole functions. The dominance of the corrections system in state government is even more evident in the fact that the Department of Corrections workforce of 16,500 represents one out of every four state employees.

The cost of incapacitation of our offenders has been enormous. In a time when moderates and conservatives have joined forces to reduce taxes and, at the same time, reduce the size of government, correctional systems are demanding huge increases in both operating budgets and the capital expenditures required to build new facilities. Law enforcement–minded officials in state after state are being forced to reconcile the competing interests of corrections and other needed state services. In 1995, Oklahoma state senator Carl Hobson noted that prisons had received larger increases than any other state agency. He observed that, ". . . It's getting more and more difficult to find enough money for every state need." In 1998, Michigan state senator John Schwarz, chairman

> *"Public officials everywhere have adopted the blunt philosophy . . . that life in prison should be ' . . . akin to a walk through the fires of hell.'"*

of the Senate Appropriations Subcommittee for Higher Education, stated emphatically, "I won't vote for a corrections budget that has one penny more in new money than what goes to universities." In California, the university system's capital expansion program was put on hold as billions of dollars were directed to pay for the construction of new prisons. Examples of this nature can be found in virtually every region of the country.

The "Get Tough" Approach

As the public continues to demand that something be done about the perception of runaway crime, politicians and public officials are refocusing attention on the cheaper and the more attention-grabbing issue of prison conditions and programs. Public officials everywhere have adopted the blunt philosophy of former Massachusetts Governor William Weld, who, in April 1998, at then Attorney General William Barr's *Summit on Corrections*, stated that life in prison should be ". . . akin to a walk through the fires of hell."

Recognizing the fiscal reality that expansion of prisons, if left unchecked, will eventually bankrupt a state's ability to provide other needed services and programs, legislative and political leaders turned to this "get tough" approach to prison operations. The opinions of Michigan state representative Mike Goschka are reflective of attitudes nationally. During a debate on prisoner conditions he stated, "Prisoners have it too easy now. They got color TV's, weight lifting equipment, libraries. . . . We need to return to the concept that prison is not fun." Many, like Rep. Goschka and Governor Weld, have adopted the theory that the most effective way to prevent crime is to make the punishment so harsh and so certain that those who are considering a life of crime will decide that the risk is not worth taking. The concept of these leaders is simple: Remove prison perks and save money while enhancing punishment, "Make 'em break rocks" has become a cornerstone in the criminal justice agenda for many elected officials. More important, it is viewed by a large segment of the public as an effective and appropriate means of fighting crime in the United States.

Examples of this strategy can be found across the country in almost every jurisdiction. In February 1998, the California Department of Corrections initiated steps to revoke a number of privileges, including weight lifting equipment. A spokesperson for then Governor Pete Wilson, in explaining the basis for many of the changes in policy, stated that prisoners are ". . . there to be punished, and hopefully rehabilitated. . . . They're not there to be entertained and catered to." Similar debates occurred in Congress over the use of weights in the Federal Bureau of Prisons. In Michigan, state representative David Jaye advocated "hot bunking," the practice of sleeping in shifts on the same bunk. He stated that, "We could double the prisoner capacity at the existing prisons by instituting two different sleeping shifts." A colleague of Jaye's introduced legislation that would ban television and radio from state prisons and all county jails. In introducing his legislation he cited Florida as a state that had already implemented such a ban on televisions.

Weighing Policies vs. Impact

In jurisdiction after jurisdiction, there has been a call to eliminate everything with the perception of being less than "tough." Law libraries, educational programs, weight lifting equipment, televisions, vocational training programs, access to medical care, food service, personal property, uniforms, and visits are among those aspects of prison life singled out in some way as needing to be reformed or eliminated in their entirety. At the same time, public officials have demanded implementation of chain gangs, pink uniforms, hard labor, hot bunking, food loafs (a loaf made of all foods prepared for that meal, served to prisoners who have thrown food at staff or other inmates), and other punitive measures.

Correctional administrators are caught squarely in the middle of this national debate. As prison populations have grown and double bunking (two or more prisoners in a cell) has become the norm, prisons have become more difficult to manage. Administrators have seen the need to evaluate every aspect of prison operations and to implement policies and procedures that address the new demands the changing population has placed on prison staff.

Reductions in personal property, revised visitation rules, and placing prisoners in uniforms are among the policy changes supported by a number of experienced correctional administrators. These measures are supported by administrators, however, not out of a desire to be punitive, but to enhance the safety and security of the facilities they manage, For example, restrictions in access to and quantities of personal property are necessitated by the size and demographics of the population.

> *"Change that is viewed [by inmates] as unwarranted and punitive is often met with resistance."*

Changes based on sound, well thought out correctional policy are significantly different from legislative edicts based on the new "get tough" attitudes of many public officials. Correctional administrators must weigh the benefits of policy change against the potential impact these changes may have on the stability of the institutions they manage. Public officials often view the impact on the prison environment as secondary to their goal of providing a solution to a very complicated issue.

> *"There is growing concern that prisons, and particularly the new wave of punitive measures, may turn nonviolent offenders into violent offenders."*

The modern prison environment is a complex and reactionary being. Change that is viewed as unwarranted and punitive is often met with resistance and, in the worst case, violence. Correctional administrators must consider that reality when implementing new policies. Public officials proposing tough measures often times neither understand nor are worried about the consequences. Don Novey, president of the California Correctional Peace Officers Association, expressed the concern of the correctional officers his union represents when he stated that ". . . You're massively overcrowded. . . . You're understaffed. . . . And this stuff goes to the forefront. It's stupid. But it resonates with the public. We get this perception that we're tough. . . ." Similarly, Pat Keohene, president of the North American Association of Wardens and Superintendents, expressed the frustration and concern of many correctional professionals when he said, ". . . When it comes to managing prisons, no one has all the answers, but someone should have the courtesy to seek our opinions before they pass these laws."

Creating Meaner Inmates

The concern that we are attempting to resolve the issue of violence in America at the expense of creating violence and tension in our prisons is real. Many feel that these punitive measures place the correctional staff and the prisoners they manage at risk. But perhaps even more important is the potential that these measures have to increase the very problem they attempt to address. Will the toughening and hardening of our prisons actually create a meaner and more isolated offender who will return to society seeking to get even? John Irwin, retired sociology professor at San Francisco State University, expressed his support for that concern when he stated that ". . . convicts come out and they're enraged."

The minimum goals of any correctional administrator include the desire that no one leave their custody worse off than when they entered. But one can't help being concerned about the lasting impact that programs such as forced participation in chain gangs might have on an already potentially violent offender. What will be the long-term consequences of forcing offenders to wear pink underwear and to eat food loaf for no other reason than to be punitive? Alvin Bronstein of the American Civil Liberty Union's National Prison Project expressed his concern over the ". . . spirit of meanness, selfishness and punitiveness that seems to have no bounds."

How much punishment is enough and at what point is it counterproductive?

This is an old question that needs a fresh look in view of the changing attitudes of America toward punishment and prisons. Criminologist Dennis J. Stevens asserts that the adage, "violence begets violence," holds true in prisons also. In one study he found that inmates who had been subjected to less volatile prison environments expressed less interest in re-offending upon release. Harsh enforcement of rules caused more disciplinary problems and resistance to rules, rather than compliance.

There is growing concern that prisons, and particularly the new wave of punitive measures, may turn nonviolent offenders into violent offenders. Public officials should seek out the advice and counsel of experienced correctional administrators before passing legislative mandates that significantly alter prison environments. Arthur Schlesinger, Jr. once said that "Politics is about the search for remedy." Legislative and public officials engaged in the national debate over the toughening of our prisons need to step back and analyze the consequences of the "make 'em break rocks" movement, and determine if it is generating a remedy to the national problem of crime and violence or creating an environment in which violence will be sustained and enhanced.

Supermaximum Security Prisons Are Necessary for Violent Offenders

by Gerald Berge, Jeffrey Geiger, and Scot Whitney

About the authors: *Gerald Berge is warden of the Wisconsin Supermax Correctional Institution. Jeffrey Geiger is director of the Justice Group at Arnold and O'Sheridan, Inc., an engineering firm that designs prisons. Scot Whitney is a mechanical engineer at Arnold and O'Sheridan.*

Every state correctional system has them: inmates who go beyond the conceivable, who are always at their worst and who are most devious and manipulative. Wisconsin is no exception.

As a result, Wisconsin opened its first supermax correctional facility in 1999 in Boscobel to house the most disruptive violent offenders. The Wisconsin Supermax Correctional Institution can house up to 500 inmates, separating them from the general inmate population, one another and the public.

Isolating Disruptive Inmates

Disruptive inmate activity and disturbances at general population correctional facilities were on the rise in Wisconsin during the late 1980s and early 1990s. Situations were becoming increasingly more dangerous for staff and inmates. Consequently, the state determined it needed an additional deterrent—a behavior management tool secure enough to give even the most challenging inmates reason to pause and change their long-established behavior patterns. The task was clear: Do what is necessary to securely house the most difficult inmates while keeping staff and the public safe and allowing inmates the chance to change.

The safety of both inmates and staff was at stake. The state's vision was matched with creative thinking. A "team-think" approach was conceived to allow correctional system veterans, technology experts and facility operations experts to share their knowledge and experience. That collective input was the basis for designing the supermax facility.

The supermax is designed to provide the highest level of security and the most controlled movement for the most troublesome inmates. There are five 100-cell housing units, each divided into groups of 25 cells called ranges. Cell fronts are configured in a linear design facing each other in a secure corridor. The ranges are configured around a local control station. One unit is high-security, one is transitional and the remaining three are general security.

> *"The supermax is designed to provide the highest level of security . . . for the most troublesome inmates."*

The supermax is surrounded by an electrified perimeter fence, which is the first line of defense for threats from the outside and the last for threats from the inside. The system consists of two 12-foot fences with razor ribbon and an electrified fence in between. The electrified fence is capable of operating in two modes—stun, which is designed to deter penetration, but not injure, and lethal, which is designed to administer a lethal shock. The system is normally in stun mode and is switched to the lethal mode by a perimeter intrusion system or by an elevated observation post. These systems are interfaced to the facility wide security control and monitoring system. There is no grass inside the perimeter fence.

Cameras mounted around the exterior of the fence and around the perimeter of the main building within the fence are programmed to respond to the zone in alarm and cameras will automatically pan, tilt and zoom to the zone in alarm. These cameras are monitored at central control and at the elevated observation post.

Central Control

The supermax was designed around a core of technology integration that literally begins at the front door. Biometric identification systems verify the identity of every person—inmates, staff, visitors and emergency personnel—who enters the supermax. The biometric system combines hand-scanning, digital photography and personal identification numbers in a secure digital database. Everyone must have his or her identity confirmed upon admission.

Technology is present throughout the entire facility. The security system includes integration of the perimeter fence, door control, door monitoring, multiple intercom systems, video surveillance, motion detection and exterior lighting.

In addition, mechanical, electrical, plumbing, smoke-control, structural systems and architectural elements are interrelated to enhance safety and security. System redundancy and integration were the keys to making this facility a correctional bastion.

At the core is central control—a kind of fortress within a fortress in which multiple technologies monitor inmate security and staff safety. Officers at central control monitor interactions between staff and inmates. Dual stations at central control provide control for every action within the supermax. A totally integrated electronics system provides a redundant security system that is a unique combination of motion-sensing cameras, specially configured programmable logic controllers and a custom-configured software control system. All alarms and actions are recorded to a dedicated computer in central control by date and time stamping to the hard drive. This provides a history trail if a condition occurs that requires investigation.

Monitors at central control allow staff to monitor and record movement both inside and outside the facility. Pan, tilt and zoom controls allow staff to control image detail. Any camera within the supermax can be linked to a videocassette recorder. All cell plumbing systems can be controlled at central control as well. Water flow, duration and control can be monitored and adjusted. Systems are designed to prevent simultaneous flushing.

A hardwired, wall-mounted redundant graphic annunciator, or duplicate-lit control panel, at central control gives staff an at-a-glance picture of activity within the entire facility—every door that opens or closes within the defined perimeter. This unique system gives a clear picture of all activity without having to scroll a graphic on a monitor, ultimately reducing an emergency team's response time for a situation within the facility. Central control also hosts a fire alarm graphic control computer, which can pinpoint the exact device in alarm and the location. In case of emergency, riot control doors and smoke curtains can segregate the facility into different segments, allowing time for emergency team members to respond. In addition to central control, each unit has its own local control station in which inmate activity can be monitored, video can be recorded 24 hours per day and cell intercom calls are answered.

> *"Restricted phone calls and visits . . . and interaction with other inmates are . . . considered deterrents from bad behavior."*

Meeting the State's Vision

The state's vision for the supermax facility resulted in three clear goals: ensure constant contact between correctional officers and central control, allow no controlling keys within cell units and provide the ability to constantly monitor officer-inmate interactions. The combination of innovative technology and the best of correctional practices provided the security basis needed at the supermax.

All correctional officers are in constant communication with central control by one or more of three methods—a secure telephone system, a secure radio system or a security intercom system dedicated to security communications. Correctional officers at the supermax typically travel in pairs and each officer has a direct communications link available to him or her at all times. Officers also are monitored by motion-sensing cameras as they proceed through inmate-occupied areas. Transactions between staff and inmates can be viewed and recorded by video to confirm safety and security.

Cells are arranged in a linear design in groups of 25 cells known as ranges. Doors to each range, unit and cell, as well as any other doors within the prison's secure perimeter, are centrally controlled. There are no controlling keys within any of the housing units or ranges. The only keys are signal keys, which are located at each cell. A signal key is a switch that directs central control to the location to be accessed, but does not actually unlock a particular door. Each key signal then is confirmed by audio via ceiling-mounted speakers or intercom stations and visual verification via cameras. The door is remotely opened by central control.

The state's goal was to have the capability to monitor and record most activities at the supermax. Interactions between inmates and staff are videotaped. Every cell in the supermax can be made camera-ready. More than 165 cameras and more than 400 miles of cabling securely monitor the facility.

Why Supermax?

The supermax is the last resort for many inmates who are disruptive in other correctional settings. It is a behavior management tool and is not a facility where most inmates would serve their entire sentences. The supermax operates on the philosophy of increased incentives for appropriate behavior: Inmates "earn" their way into the supermax by disrupting the normal operations of other correctional institutions and earn their way out by demonstrating acceptable behavior with increased privileges.

Privileges at the supermax are limited—restricted phone calls and visits, monitored exercise time and interaction with other inmates are all considered deterrents from bad behavior. Inmates are moved through a system of levels, earning their way through the different levels of the supermax program.

When inmates are transported to the supermax, they are brought in through a vehicle-secure sally port. Inmates begin their stay with a base evaluation at the highest level of security. As an inmate's behavior complies, he (currently the facility is just for male offenders) is moved through security levels eventually entering the transitional unit before being reintroduced to a general correctional population. Inmates who earn their way to the transitional unit are allowed small group contact with other inmates and staff to prepare them for reintroduction into the general population.

> *"Most inmates are confined to their cells for the majority of each day."*

Once inside, personal contact is controlled. The supermax is designed to maximize monitoring capabilities. Each cell is capable of being equipped with audio and video systems to monitor inmate activity. Cells also are equipped with individual smoke detectors tied into a master smoke control system. All security-sensitive electronic equipment is located outside maximum-detention zones.

Cell accommodations are basic—a mattress on top of a concrete bed, a wall-mounted writing table, a wall-mounted electronics shelf, shower, drain and combination toilet/wash basin. The high-security cells have two pneumatically operated doors that control access. Cell configuration controls inmate interaction and the passing of contraband. A cell intercom call system was developed using a nonmechanical push button with the principles of static electricity to deter inmate vandalism.

> *"The supermax has fulfilled its goals and is succeeding as a tool for its users."*

Nonprofessional visitors, other than inmates' lawyers, visit offenders through a video visitation system. Only official guests are allowed to enter the supermax's secure perimeter. A video visitation area also is provided in the gatehouse.

The supermax has an on-site medical facility with specially monitored medical cells. The feature allows staff to meet many inmate medical needs without transferring them to another institution. Also, a telecommunications video system provides telemedicine.

Most inmates are confined to their cells for the majority of each day with services brought to them. Except for transition inmates, that includes meals and all educational programming. Inmate movement outside the cell is limited. When inmates are moved to another part of the facility, they are fully restrained. . . .

Planning Considerations

Prison life for inmates and staff alike is hazardous. Every system in the supermax, which needs to handle an extreme of abuse, was integrated to reinforce security. After all, no one in corrections skimps on security. The team that designed the supermax met early in the project process to listen to the requirements and develop practical, innovative and economically responsible solutions for a rigorous environment. . . .

There is no single factor that makes a project like the supermax facility a success. It is a combination of factors. Simply throwing expensive technology at a facility is not a good solution. The design team needs to know what technology works and how technology is used, especially in helping to control violent offenders. In a project such as this one, there are no options for afterthoughts. In a truly integrated facility the team needs to have the foresight and insight to provide the user with the information necessary to make educated decisions early in the process. The supermax has fulfilled its goals and is succeeding as a tool for its users. The supermax is an example of a successful concept becoming a successful reality.

Supermaximum Security Prisons Are Inhumane

by Sasha Abramsky

About the author: *Sasha Abramsky is the author of* Hard Time Blues, *an examination of America's growing prison system.*

Last summer [2001], some 600 inmates in the notorious supermaximum-security unit at California's Pelican Bay State Prison [in northern California] stopped eating. They were protesting the conditions in which the state says it must hold its most difficult prisoners: locked up for 23 hours out of every 24 in a barren concrete cell measuring 7½ by 11 feet. One wall of these cells is perforated steel; inmates can squint out through the holes, but there's nothing to see outside either. In Pelican Bay's supermax unit, as in most supermax prisons around the country, the cells are arranged in lines radiating out like spokes from a control hub, so that no prisoner can see another human being—except for those who are double-bunked. Last year [2001], the average population of the Pelican Bay supermax unit was 1,200 inmates, and on average, 288 men shared their tiny space with a "cellie." Since 1995, 12 double-bunked prisoners in the Pelican Bay supermax unit have been murdered by their cell mates. But near-total isolation is the more typical condition.

Extreme Deprivation

Meals are slid to the inmates through a slot in the steel wall. Some prisoners are kept in isolation even for the one hour per day that they're allowed out to exercise; all are shackled whenever they are taken out of their cells. And many are forced to live this way for years on end.

Such extreme deprivation, the food strikers said, literally drives people crazy. Many experts agree. But the protest died out after two weeks, according to the jailhouse lawyer who organized it; and though a state senator promised that he would look into the strikers' complaints, so far conditions at Pelican Bay remain unchanged.

Sasha Abramsky, "Return of the Madhouse: Supermax Prisons Are Becoming the High-Tech Equivalent of the Nineteenth-Century Snake Pit," *The American Prospect*, vol. 13, February 11, 2002, pp. 26–29.

All told, more than 8,000 prisoners in California and at least 42,000 around the country, by the conservative estimate of the *Corrections Yearbook*, are currently held in similar conditions of extreme confinement. As of 2000, Texas alone boasted 16 supermax prisons and supermax units, housing some 10,000 inmates. In Florida, more than 7,000 inmates were double-bunked in such facilities and the corrections department was lobbying to build another one (at an estimated cost of nearly $50 million) to house an additional 1,000 offenders.

"The chances for guard-on-inmate violence remain high at . . . supermaxes around the country."

Seven years ago, in January 1995, inmates at Pelican Bay won a class-action lawsuit, *Madrid v. Gomez*, against the California Department of Corrections. Among other constitutional violations, U.S. District Court Judge Thelton Henderson found that the staff had systematically brutalized inmates, particularly mentally ill inmates. "The Eighth Amendment's restraint on using excessive force has been repeatedly violated at Pelican Bay, leading to a conspicuous pattern of excessive force," Henderson wrote in describing the severe beatings then common at the facility, the third-degree burns inflicted on one mentally ill inmate who was thrown into boiling water after he smeared himself with feces, and the routine use of painful restraining weapons against others. The judge ordered California to remove any seriously mentally ill or retarded inmates from the supermax unit, and he appointed a special master to overhaul the prison.

What Henderson didn't rule, however, was that the supermax model, per se, amounted to cruel and unusual punishment in violation of the Eighth Amendment. And so, while a new warden and new rules were brought to Pelican Bay, the basic conditions of sensory deprivation in its supermax unit have remained intact. Extremely mentally ill inmates are now held elsewhere; but critics say that less severe cases are still sent to the unit, where they often deteriorate drastically, for the same reasons that Judge Henderson originally identified: "The physical environment reinforces a sense of isolation and detachment from the outside world, and helps create a palpable distance from ordinary compunctions, inhibitions and community norms."

Meanwhile, the prescribed method for dealing with uncooperative inmates who "act out" in a supermax is still to send a team of guards into the cell with batons, stun guns, Mace, and tear gas. Thus, say critics, the chances for guard-on-inmate violence remain high at Pelican Bay, just as at other supermaxes around the country.

Roots of the Supermax Model

The supermax model emerged out of the prison violence of the 1970s and the early 1980s, when dozens of guards around the country, including two at the maximum-security federal prison at Marion, Illinois, were murdered by prisoners. First, prison authorities developed procedures to minimize inmate-staff contact; then they took to "locking down" entire prisons for indefinite periods, keeping inmates in their cells all day and closing down communal dining rooms and exercise yards. Eventually, they began to explore the idea of making the general prison population safer by creating entirely separate high-tech, supermax prisons in which "the worst of the worst" gang leaders and sociopaths would be incarcerated in permanent lockdown conditions. In the late 1980s, several states and the federal government began constructing supermax units. California—which had seen 11 guards murdered by inmates between 1970 and 1973, and a staggering 32 prisoners killed by other inmates in 1972 alone—opened Corcoran State Prison and its supermax unit in 1988 and Pelican Bay the year following. In 1994 the first federal supermax opened, in Florence, Colorado. Soon, dozens of correctional systems across the country were embracing this model.

Indeed, throughout the 1990s, despite year-by-year declines in crime, one state after another pumped tens of millions of dollars into building supermax prisons and supermax facilities within existing prisons—sections that are usually called "secure housing units," or SHUs. Defenders of supermaxes, like Todd Ishee, warden of Ohio State Penitentiary (OSP), a supermax in Youngstown, argue that their restrictions provide a way to establish control in what is still—and inherently—an extremely dangerous environment. "In 1993," he says, "our maximum security prison at Southern Ohio Correctional Facility was host to a riot. One correctional officer was killed. A number of inmates were killed and several injured. Following the riot, the department made a decision that a 500-bed facility of this nature was needed to control the most dangerous inmates."

> *"For . . . tough-on-crime America, imposing grim conditions on [supermax] prisoners is all too often seen as a good in itself."*

Overusing Supermax Facilities

But while it may be necessary to maintain such restricted facilities as prisons of last resort for some inmates, critics point out that far less troublesome inmates end up being sent to them. In Ohio, for example, a special legislative committee appointed to inspect the state's prisons in 1999 concluded that fewer than half of the inmates at OSP met the state's own supermax guidelines. State correctional-department data indicate that of the more than 350 inmates currently incarcerated at OSP, 20 were ringleaders of the 1993 riot and 31 had killed either an inmate or a correctional officer while living among the general prison population; but the rest had been sent there for much less serious offenses (often little more than a fistfight with another inmate).

And Ohio isn't alone in this practice. According to a study issued by the state of Florida, fully one-third of the correctional departments across the country that operate supermax prisons report placing inmates in them simply because they don't have enough short-term disciplinary housing in lower-security prisons. Given that the supermaxes' average cost to taxpayers is about $50,000 per inmate per year—compared with $20,000 to $30,000 for lower-security prisons—this is hardly an economically efficient arrangement.

Yet the available numbers suggest that casual overuse of these facilities is common. For in tough-on-crime America, imposing grim conditions on prisoners is all too often seen as a good in itself, regardless of the long-term costs. The U.S. Department of Justice's 1997 report on supermax housing . . . found Mississippi officials insisting that they needed to house fully 20 percent of their prison inmates in separate supermax-type prisons and another 35 percent in similar units within existing prisons. Arizona claimed that it needed to house 8 percent of its inmates in supermax prisons and another 20 percent in SHUs. In Virginia, after Jim Austin, the state's nationally renowned consultant on prisoner classification, told officials that they needed to put more of their inmates into medium security prisons, the state instead spent approximately $150 million to build Red Onion and Wallens Ridge, two supermax prisons with a combined capacity to house 2,400 prisoners.

Proponents of the supermax system claim that its introduction has reduced violence in the general prison population—both by removing the most hard-core miscreants and also by introducing a fearsome deterrent to misbehavior. But the data on this are, at best, mixed. Among Ohio's total prison population, for example, there were more inmate-on-inmate assaults serious enough to be written up by officials in 2000 than there were in 1997, the year before the OSP supermax opened for business (8 assaults for every 1,000 prisoners in 1997 compared with 10 for every 1,000 in 2000). And even where lower-security prisons have been made somewhat safer, that safety has been purchased at a staggering financial and, ultimately, social cost.

Mental Illness

Even the best-run of the supermax facilities seem to see high rates of mental illness among their inmates. For example, a study carried out by the Washington State Department of Corrections, which is known as one of the more humane, rehabilitation-focused prison systems in the country, found that approximately 30 percent of inmates in its supermax units show evidence of serious psychiatric disorders—at least twice the rate in the overall prison population.

> *"Even the best-run of the supermax facilities seem to see high rates of mental illness among their inmates."*

In Connecticut's Northern Correctional Institution (NCI), Warden Larry Myers presides over an inmate population just shy of 500 and a staff of just over 300. With six mental-health professionals, a gradated three-phase program offering inmates the possibility of returning to the general prison population within one year, and relatively calm inmate-staff relations, Myers prides himself on running a tight ship. Unlike staffers at many other supermaxes, once those at NCI identify an inmate as psychotic, they remove him to an institution that caters to mentally ill prisoners. Myers says that to avoid a "ping-pong effect," with inmates bouncing back and forth between NCI and mental-health institutions, the prison has not accepted severely disturbed inmates since 1999.

> *"Correctional bureaucrats have devised a systematically humiliating and . . . dehumanizing regimen of punishments for [supermax] prisoners."*

Yet even in Myers's prison, psychiatrist Paul Chaplin estimates that 10 percent of the inmates are on antidepressants or antipsychotic drugs, and several times a month an inmate gets violent enough to be placed in four-point restraints. Last September [2001], guards had to subdue prisoners with Mace on 12 occasions. As I toured the pink-painted steel tiers of level one, dozens of inmates began screaming out their often incoherent complaints in a bone-jarring cacophony of despair.

"This is shitty," shouted one of the more intelligible of them. "We ain't got no recreations, no space. If I try to sit back and motivate, you got people yelling." He said he sleeps for more than 10 hours a day, does push-ups, and sits around. "I have trouble concentrating," he yelled. Through the narrow Plexiglas window in the door of his cell, a 21-year-old shouted: "I'm in jail for behavior problems. My cellie has behavior problems. Why put two people with behavior problems in the same cell?"

The greatly disputed chicken-and-egg question is: Do previously healthy inmates go mad under these extreme conditions of confinement, or do inmates who are already mentally unstable and impulsive commit disciplinary infractions that get them shipped off to SHUs or supermax prisons, where they are then likely to further decompensate?

Some psychiatrists, including Harvard University professor Stuart Grassian, have testified in court that the sensory deprivation in a supermax frequently leads otherwise healthy individuals to develop extreme manifestations of psychosis, such as hallucinations, uncontrollable rage, paranoia, and nearly catatonic depressions. Grassian and others have also documented examples of extreme self-mutilation: supermax inmates gouging out their eyes or cutting off their genitals. Using the tools of the supermax prison, writes James Gilligan in his book *Violence*, "does not protect the public; it only sends a human time bomb into the community" when the inmate is eventually released.

Other psychiatrists are more cautious, arguing that while some perfectly healthy people are driven insane by these dehumanizing prison settings, the more common problem is that mildly mentally ill inmates are often precisely the ones who find it hardest to control their behavior while in the general prison population and who therefore get sent to the supermax or SHU. Judge Henderson acknowledged this in his Pelican Bay ruling; and in *Ruiz v. Johnson*, a 1999 case involving Texas's use of long-term inmate-segregation fatalities in its prisons, another federal court likewise found that "inmates, obviously in need of medical help, are instead inappropriately managed merely as miscreants."

Dehumanizing Treatment

In the large supermaxes of Texas, correctional bureaucrats have devised a systematically humiliating and, indeed, dehumanizing regimen of punishments for prisoners who elsewhere would more likely be considered disturbed: no real meals, only a "food loaf" of all the day's food ground together, for prisoners who don't return their food trays; paper gowns forced on those who won't wear their clothes. I myself have heard guards joking about "the mutilators" who slash their own veins to get attention. According to Thomas Conklin, a psychiatrist and medical director at the Hampden County Jail in Massachusetts who was called on to evaluate mental-health care in one Texas supermax, "All suicide gestures by inmates [were] seen as manipulating the correctional system with the conscious intent of secondary gain. In not one case was the inmate's behavior seen as reflecting mental pathology that could be treated." In most supermaxes, this kind of thinking still seems to be the norm.

> *"The moral critique is this: [supermax prisons] have been designed, at the best, with utter disregard for human misery."*

Although prison authorities say that they provide mental-health care to their supermax inmates, prisoner advocates tend to dismiss these claims. Documentary-film maker Jim Lipscomb, who has interviewed scores of inmates in Ohio's most secure prisons, reports that mental-health programs there often consist of little more than in-cell videos offering such platitudes as "If you feel angry at one of the guards, try not to curse and shout at him."

"That's called mental health!" Lipscomb says in amazement.

"The forceful rushes of this isolational perversion has pulled my essence into a cesspool," wrote one inmate from a supermax in Pennsylvania to Bonnie Kerness of the American Friends Service Committee (AFSC). "This just ain't life, pathologized in a subsumed litany of steel and cement codes preoccupied with the disturbing thrust of death." Accompanying the florid words was a penciled image of a grown man curled into a fetal position against a brick wall.

Challenging the Conditions

The American Civil Liberties Union's National Prison Project is currently spearheading three class action lawsuits against supermaxes in Illinois, Ohio, and Wisconsin. In the Wisconsin case, U.S. District Court Judge Barbara Crabb issued a preliminary ruling in October [2001] against the Supermax Correctional Institute in Boscobel after hearing the testimony of various health experts, including Dr. Terry Kupers, a Berkeley psychiatrist and author of the book *Prison Madness*. Kupers, who had been to Boscobel, told me that "there're a lot of crazy people in here, and they need to be removed on an emergency basis because it's not safe." In court, he testified that he had interviewed inmates who had been diagnosed with paranoid schizophrenia and who continued to hallucinate despite being given high doses of Thorazine.

Judge Crabb ordered prison authorities to remove five mentally ill inmates from the facility immediately and to provide an independent mental-health assessment to any inmate with symptoms of mental illness. "The conditions at Supermax are so severe and restrictive," Crabb wrote, "that they exacerbate the symptoms that mentally ill inmates exhibit. Many of the severe conditions serve no legitimate penological interest; they can only be considered punishment for punishment's sake." She also set a trial date in July 2002 to hear evidence on the lawsuit's larger claim that the stringent conditions of confinement at the supermax—the extreme isolation, extraordinary levels of surveillance, and tight restrictions on personal property—constitute cruel and unusual punishment.

For advocates of prisoners' rights, this is the Holy Grail: a broad new reading of the Eighth Amendment that would prohibit supermax-style incarceration. And a broad reading is warranted, they say, by the international conventions that the United States has signed—such as the International Covenant on Civil and Political Rights and the United Nations' Standard Minimum Rules for Treatment of Prisoners, which prohibit torture and regulate prison conditions much more stringently than does U.S. case law. It's also a matter of human decency, says attorney Jamie Fellner of Human Rights Watch. "The moral critique is this: Secure-housing units have been designed, at the best, with utter disregard for human misery. At the worst, it's a deliberate use of human misery for deterrence and punishment."

Pending such a ruling, however, the filing of lawsuits provides virtually the only public accountability for what goes on in the supermaxes. With the exception of the New York Correctional Association, there is no legislatively mandated oversight agency watching the prisons—no civilian review board or independent ombudsman—in any state with supermax facilities. And over the past few years, in response to a rash of critical media coverage and unfavorable reports by human-rights organizations, many prison authorities have stopped allowing outside observers to visit these prisons or interview their inmates. (In the past, I have visited supermax sites in California, Texas, and Illinois to report on them. For this [viewpoint], only Connecticut opened its super-

> *"Evidence suggests that many [supermax] prisoners have been made more violent by their long-term spells of extreme deprivation and isolation."*

max doors to me; Arizona, New Jersey, Pennsylvania, Texas, and Virginia all refused to do so.) Says Human Rights Watch's Fellner: "It is incredible that it's sometimes easier to get access to prisons in closed regimes in third-world countries than it is in the U.S."

Breeding Violence

If nothing else, the lawsuits are keeping the human-rights questions on the table. Supermax critics are also trying to call attention to the public costs, which are not just financial. Tens of thousands of inmates are now being held in supermax facilities, and almost all of them will be released one day. Indeed, many states are releasing such inmates directly from the SHUs to the streets after their sentence is up, without even reacclimatizing them to a social environment.

Although no national tracking surveys of ex-supermax and ex-SHU inmates have been carried out, anecdotal evidence suggests that many prisoners have been made more violent by their long-term spells of extreme deprivation and isolation. Bonnie Kerness of the AFSC talks about a whole new generation of cons coming out of supermax prisons with hair-trigger tempers. One former inmate at Rikers Island jail in New York City, who now participates in a rehabilitation program run by the Manhattan-based Fortune Society, recalls that prisoners routinely referred to "Bing monsters." (The Bing is the nickname for the Rikers Island version of the SHU.)

"The impact on society could be devastating," says Steve Rigg, a former correctional officer who worked at California's supermax prison in Corcoran during the mid-1990s and blew the whistle on his fellow officers for organizing fights between rival prison-gang members. Corcoran's administration was overhauled after this, but Rigg warns that the underlying dangers in undermonitored supermaxes remain. "There's more [inmate] recidivism," he says of SHUs. "They breed the worst."

Inmates Will Benefit from Anti-Rape Legislation

by Robert W. Dumond

About the author: *Robert W. Dumond is a clinical mental health counselor who serves as an adviser to the organization Stop Prisoner Rape.*

Editor's Note: The following viewpoint was originally given as a statement before the U.S. Senate on July 31, 2002, in support of the Prison Rape Reduction Act.

The scourge of prisoner sexual assault was recognized early in the history of U.S. corrections when the Rev. Louis Dwight of the Boston Discipline Society condemned this "dreadful degradation" in 1826. While most Americans know it is a problem, no national database exists, and the actual extent of prison sexual assault is not precisely known. In 35 years, there have been less than 16 published studies conducted to accurately assess its epidemiology, only three of which have included data about women prisoners. We do, however, have a reliable baseline of incidence data from two large-scale studies of Midwestern prison systems recently conducted by Cindy Struckman-Johnson and her colleagues. She found that:

- 22 to 25% of prisoners are the victims of sexual pressuring, attempted sexual assault, or completed rapes.
- 1 in 10 (10%) prisoners is the victim of a completed rape at least one time during the course of his or her incarceration.
- ⅔ of those reporting sexual victimization have been victimized repeatedly— an average of nine times during their incarceration—with some male prisoners experiencing up to 100 incidents of sexual assault per year.

All Inmates Are Vulnerable

Using this data, it is reasonable to assume that in states with larger, heterogeneous urban populations, the rates of sexual assault are even higher. This assumption is supported by the study of one California medium security prison

Robert W. Dumond, statement before the Senate Committee on the Judiciary, Washington, DC, July 31, 2002.

which found that 1 in 7 inmates (14%) reported being sexually victimized. In fact, many scholars agree with the admonishment of Drs. D.J. Cotton and A.N. Groth "that available statistics must be regarded as very conservative at best, since discovery and documentation of this behavior are compromised by the nature of prison conditions, inmate codes and subculture and staff attitudes." One of the goals of the *Prison Rape Reduction Act* is to scientifically collect and validate the actual incidence of prisoner sexual assault in all correctional facilities nationwide.[1]

While *no* inmate is immune from sexual victimization, empirical evidence demonstrates that there are certain categories of male prisoners who are especially vulnerable: (a) the young and inexperienced; (b) the

> *"'Available statistics [documenting prison rape] must be regarded as very conservative at best.'"*

physically weak and small; (c) inmates suffering from mental illness or developmental disabilities; (d) inmates who are not "tough" or "street-wise"; (e) inmates who are not gang-affiliated; (f) homosexual, transgendered, or overtly effeminate inmates; (g) inmates who have violated the "code of silence"; (h) those who are disliked by staff or other inmates; and (i) inmates who have been previously sexually assaulted. Race has also been identified as a factor contributing to prison rape in settings with high racial tension. It has further been shown that targets of sexual aggression may act out violently themselves, making the transition from victim to aggressor in an effort to avoid further victimization.

For female prisoners, it is not clear which particular characteristics play a role in determining who will be targeted for sexual abuse, but first-time offenders, young women, and mentally disabled women appear to be particularly vulnerable. Custodial sexual assault has received considerable attention, as it should, and many important steps have been initiated to rectify the problem. It should be recognized, however, that in the only two empirically based studies which have been done, about half of the incidents were committed by other female inmates, and the remaining were committed by male and female custodial staff. Clearly, further study of female victimization, which this bill will provide, is warranted.

Devastating Effects

The crisis of being a sexual assault survivor is pervasive, devastating, and global—with profound physical, emotional, social, and spiritual components. The effects of such victimization in prisons and jails have been shown to be even more debilitating, due to the unique structure of incarceration that increases the impact upon victims. Incarcerated victims are more often physically assaulted during attacks, and routinely experience a systematic, repetitive in-

---

1. The Prison Rape Reduction Act, renamed the Prison Rape Elimination Act, was signed into law in September 2003.

fliction of psychological trauma, fear, helplessness, and terror as the physical/sexual abuse continues. Male victims may be marked as "punks" and forced to endure years of sexual slavery. Whatever an inmate victim chooses to do regarding the sexual assault (reporting the crime, seeking protective custody, engaging in protective pairing) has a profound impact upon his or her future while incarcerated.

The mental health consequences are catastrophic. Male and female victims often experience post-traumatic stress disorder (PTSD), anxiety, depression, and exacerbation of preexisting psychiatric disorders, and most victims are at risk of committing suicide as a means of avoiding the ongoing trauma. The problem is even mere acute when one recognizes that America's jails and prisons currently house more mentally ill than the nation's psychiatric hospitals collectively. Unfortunately, most correctional facilities are ill-prepared to provide adequate, comprehensive services to victims, who often even fail to disclose their victimization out of fear and humiliation.

The public health consequences are equally overwhelming. In addition to the devastating physical consequences of the assaults themselves, victims may contract HIV/AIDS, other sexually transmitted diseases, other communicable diseases (such as tuberculosis and hepatitis B and C, which are rampant in U.S. correctional institutions). These diseases can be spread to others in both the prison population and the general community. In addition to the possibility of disease exposure, female inmates have been impregnated as a result of staff sexual misconduct. Some of these women have further been subjected to inappropriate segregation and denied adequate health care services.

> *"Incarcerated [rape] victims . . . routinely experience . . . psychological trauma, fear, helplessness, and terror."*

Ignorance and Indifference

The mission of America's correctional institutions is to provide for the "care, custody and control" of those individuals committed to their supervision. Prisoner sexual assault destabilizes the safety and security of America's jails and prisons. For over 25 years it has been recognized as a contributing factor in prison homicides, violence against inmates/staff, and institutional insurrections and riots. Administrative and programmatic solutions, focusing on prevention, intervention and prosecution, have long been recommended by authorities, yet not implemented by the responsible officials. Strategies such as increasing surveillance of critical areas in the institution, improved classification procedures to identify potential victims and aggressors, adequate medical/mental health treatment for victims, and isolation and prosecution of offenders, have been proposed for over 20 years. Despite this, too many U.S. correctional officials have manifested either ignorance, misunderstanding, or, most alarmingly, deliberate indifference about this crisis.

In effect, prison administrators have been largely unaccountable for the prison sexual assaults committed under their watch. Some analysts have even suggested that prison sexual assaults have been used as a management tool to maintain order—a perverse and unacceptable practice.

Joanne Mariner's 2001 survey of all 50 state departments of correction and the federal Bureau of Prisons confirmed that most correctional authorities deny that the problem exists. Effective management can only be implemented using accurate data, yet only 23 out of 46 corrections departments reported that they maintain distinct statistical information on inmate sexual assault, and no state reported data consistent with the large sample surveys of Midwestern prisons. Even though there has been universal consensus that correctional staff training is vital to addressing prison rape, only six state correctional departments (Arkansas, Illinois, Massachusetts, New Hampshire, North Carolina, Virginia) and the federal Bureau of Prisons currently provide staff with such training. Criminal prosecution is virtually non-existent in cases of prisoner sexual assault. Corrections in America have considerably improved with professionalization; nevertheless, the largest correctional accreditation agency, the American Correctional Association, has no current standard regarding inmate sexual assault.

A Comprehensive Strategy

The Prison Rape Reduction Act provides a tangible, comprehensive strategy to address the complex challenges posed by prisoner sexual assault. With accurate incidence data, correctional administrators can make rational decisions about staff deployment, inmate placement, and resource allocation, thereby improving the safety and security of America's confinement institutions. Importantly, this is a crisis which can be resolved without significant monetary expenditures. The bill's emphasis on visibility and accountability will be highly effective as it mandates that accurate information be collected and maintained by correctional institutions, and provides for careful scrutiny of each facility's prison rape abatement practices. Prison officials with poor responses will be held accountable for their inaction and indifference. The National Prison Rape Reduction Commission will also play a key role by developing reasonable standards in areas such as staff training, recordkeeping, and protection for "whistle-blowers." Correctional staff will operate pursuant to the highest ethical and professional standards, and comprehensive treatment for inmate victims will begin to heal the devastating impact of sexual assault.

The human rights organization Stop Prisoner Rape has endorsed this legislation as a critical step toward curbing one of the most pervasive and devastating abuses that has been allowed to continue in our country. Stop Prisoner Rape and I urge you to support this legislation designed to address an abuse that destroys human dignity, contributes to the spread of disease, and perpetuates violence both inside and outside of prison walls. The time to address this travesty has come.

Inmates Are Not Likely to Benefit from Anti-Rape Legislation

by Robert Weisberg and David Mills

About the authors: *Robert Weisberg is the Edwin E. Huddleson Jr. professor of law at Stanford Law School. David Mills is a senior lecturer and director of clinical education at Stanford Law School.*

Imagine the following defense argument being put forth to a judge who's about to sentence a defendant—an attractive long-haired young man of small but athletic build and gentle demeanor—after he has been convicted of molesting a teenage victim:

> Your Honor, it is unfair and disproportionate to sentence my client to jail, since it will almost certainly subject him to violent and probably sexual assault while incarcerated. As the evidence we will proffer shows, there is a 50 percent chance he will suffer an aggravated assault and at least a 40 percent likelihood he will be raped and sodomized on multiple occasions while imprisoned. We thus urge you, Your Honor, to recognize that any sentence of incarceration effectively includes these "secondary" sanctions.

Superficial Anti-Rape Legislation

This motion seems fanciful, but it would be perfectly plausible for a defense lawyer to make. In fact, one wishes more defense lawyers would do so, since all these contentions are essentially true. While hard data on sexual assaults in prison is not easy to find, and observers dispute the precise frequency, no one who knows American jails and prisons doubts that rape and sexual assault— usually perpetrated by other inmates but occasionally by prison staff—are facts of daily life. What is surprising is how easily the citizenry and the judicial system have come to accept the brutal reality of our prisons and absorbed it into mainstream culture. A new bill adopted by Congress purports to address this widespread apathy toward prison brutality. But, whether or not its proponents were sincere, the bill is a superficial gesture of little substance.

This past July [2003] Congress enacted the Prison Rape Elimination Act of 2003, providing $60 million for a two-year survey of state and federal prisons to determine the pervasiveness of prison rape and creating various panels to offer remedies. Congressional sponsors of the bill included the most improbable political allies, and support for the bill ranged from the ACLU [American Civil Liberties Union] and Human Rights Watch [HRW] to conservative evangelical organizations. (The clear interest of the latter in promoting religion among inmates has helped create a strange-bedfellowship with leftist prisoners' rights groups.) The bill passed both houses unanimously, and President [George W.] Bush, flanked by two former inmates who had been raped in prison, signed it in early September. The reason you've never heard of the Prison Rape Elimination Act is probably that no one who knows our criminal justice system believes it will do much of anything to eliminate prison rape.

> *"No one who knows our criminal justice system believes [the Prison Rape Elimination Act] will . . . eliminate prison rape."*

Even the more modest earlier title for the bill—the Prison Rape Reduction Act—was an ambitious predictor of its likely outcome. Because despite its grand words and its sponsors' passionate expressions of concern, the main thing the law aims to do is collect data, and that may be, paradoxically, both quixotic and redundant.

Unreliable Rape Data

It is quixotic because the obvious problems of unreliable observations and underreporting inherent in prison assault make highly refined objective data a fantasy. It is redundant because the relevant facts are already clear: A recent report by Human Rights Watch synthesized data and various perception surveys from around the United States and *conservatively* concluded that approximately 20 percent of all inmates are sexually assaulted in some way and at least 7 percent raped. A cautious inference is that nearly 200,000 current inmates have been raped and nearly 1 million have been sexually assaulted over the past 20 years. And, as HRW notes, prisoners with certain characteristics—first offenders, those with high voices and passive or intellectual personalities—face far higher probabilities. Moreover, the reports reveal that sexual slavery following rape is also an ordinary occurrence. Stories abound of prisoners who, once they are "turned out" (prison jargon for the initial rape) become the rapists' subordinates, forced to do menial jobs and sometimes "rented out" to other inmates to satisfy their sexual needs.

Of course, prisoners face not only sexual assault from other inmates, but violence of all forms, often leading to horrific injuries and death. All too typical is the story, repeated by HRW, of a raped Texas prisoner with obvious injuries who reported the rapes (eight alleged rapes by the same rapist) to prison authorities. The authorities interviewed the rapist and the victim together, concluded it was nothing but a "lovers' quarrel," and sent them both back to their cells, where the victim was again repeatedly raped and beaten even more brutally. Also surprisingly typical is the very recent, notorious killing of Father John Geoghan, the Massachusetts priest imprisoned for sexual assault, whom the state correctional system effectively, if unintentionally, sentenced to death in a non-capital punishment jurisdiction.

Even if allocating the time and funds to collecting this additional data were somehow useful, how does the federal government propose to find it? Does the Department of Justice (DOJ), charged with overseeing the study, have some secret methodology at its disposal that it's not sharing with us? And even if all this further data collection somehow dramatizes the problem, what then? Despite promises (or threats) in the new law to take prison officials or state governments to task for failure to stop rape and assault, the real cause probably lies in a more mundane and intractable reality: Inmates will attack inmates if enough of them live in sufficient proximity, with insufficient internal security, for long enough periods of time. That means that while Congress funds lots of studies, we already know that the key variables are really the sheer rates of incarceration in the United States, the density of prison housing, the number and quality of staff, and the abandonment of any meaningful

> *"The United States has essentially accepted . . . brutal sexual violence . . . as an inevitable consequence of incarcerating criminals."*

attempts at rehabilitation. If it is honest, the new DOJ commission created by the law will suggest what we already know is necessary: that we lower incarceration rates, reduce the prisoner-to-space ratio, train huge numbers of new guards to protect prisoners, and abandon the purely retributive and incapacitative function of prisons. But there is no political will for such changes, which is perhaps why we fund studies of the obvious in the first place.

Acceptance of Violence and Assault

The truth is that the United States has essentially accepted violence—and particularly brutal sexual violence—as an inevitable consequence of incarcerating criminals. Indeed, prison assault has become a cliché within mainstream culture. The news and entertainment media refer to it nonchalantly. Prime-time TV shows, such as *Oz*, depict the most awful scenes of rape and carnage. Popular TV dramas routinely depict police taunting potential defendants with threats of the violence and sexual abuse they will face in prison. Indeed, last year 7UP ran a TV advertisement in which a teasing threat of sexual assault in prison was part of a lighthearted pitch for selling soda. The advertisement ran for two months without objection and was only pulled after criticisms from prisoners' rights groups.

So accepted is assault as part of prison life that an outsider might conclude that on some basic, if unarticulated level, we think it an appropriate element of the punishment regimen. Perhaps we believe that allowing prisons to be places of horrific acts will serve as part of the utilitarian deterrent effect of criminal sentences. Or perhaps we recognize that prison rape and assault are an unavoidable byproduct of the rape and assault in society generally, so that our goal here is not utilitarian but retributive: that is, even though we cannot eliminate rape and assault, we can at least reallocate them. Thus, when we purport to incapacitate convicted criminals, what we are really doing is shifting to them, the most "deserving" among us, the burden of victimization.

The Prison Rape Elimination Act is better than nothing—unless, of course, it represents the last gesture politicians intend to make in the direction of addressing this problem. Assuming the study does not blinker reality by denying the prevalence of the problem, it will presumably mandate or exhort state and federal officials to monitor, train, and discipline prison staff and enhance inmate security—all under a threat of withdrawal of federal funds or the firing of negligent officials. Of course, the government would thereby be implicitly forcing prison officials to spend vast amounts of money they do not have and that Congress is unlikely to give state legislatures in the first place.

Perhaps while this federal study is under way, there are other, more honest ways of acknowledging what the American prison system has created. Perhaps every sentencing judge should require that a defendant headed for prison be given extensive "pre-rape counseling" in the hope that he or she can take some small personal steps to reduce the risk of attack. Or perhaps we could require judges to demand data about the differential risks of rape and assault for different types of prisoners in different prisons and begin to factor such data into any sentence. "You committed murder, so let's send you somewhere where you're *really* likely to be raped." In that way we will be at least as brutally honest with ourselves as we are literally brutal with our prisoners.

Inmate Health Care Must Be Improved

by the National Commission on Correctional Health Care

About the author: *The National Commission on Correctional Health Care is a nonprofit organization committed to improving the quality of health care in jails, prisons, and juvenile detention facilities.*

The inmate population in the United States has been growing rapidly since the early 1970s: As of 1999, an estimated 2 million persons were incarcerated in the Nation's jails and prisons compared with 325,400 in 1970—an increase of almost 600 percent. Approximately 11.5 million inmates were released into the community in 1998, most from city and county jails. . . . These inmates are at higher risk for many serious diseases and mental illness than are nonincarcerated individuals.

Inmates and Communicable Diseases

- The prevalence rates for several serious communicable diseases are significantly higher among inmates and releasees than in the total U.S. population. Seventeen percent of the estimated 229,000 persons living with AIDS in the country in 1996 passed through a correctional facility that year. An extremely high 29–32 percent of the estimated 4.5 million people infected with hepatitis C in 1996 in the United States served time in prison or jail that year.

- Inmates have high rates of some serious chronic diseases, including asthma, diabetes, and hypertension. Prevalence rates for asthma are higher among inmates than among the total U.S. population.

- The prevalence of mental illness is higher among inmates than among the rest of the population. An estimated 2.3 to nearly 4 percent of inmates in State prisons have schizophrenia or another psychosis compared with 0.8 percent among the population of the Nation as a whole.

National Commission on Correctional Health Care, *The Health Status of Soon-to-Be-Released Inmates*, vol. 1, March 2002, pp. 2–5.

These high rates of communicable disease, chronic disease, and mental illness among an expanding inmate population create a critical need for prevention, screening, and treatment services before these individuals are released into the community. Why? First, serious diseases affecting inmates can be transmitted to other inmates. Absent appropriate screening and isolation for contagious individuals, tuberculosis (TB) transmission is a serious possibility in prisons and jails because of poor ventilation and overcrowding. HIV transmission has been documented within correctional facilities, albeit at low rates. In addition, the many inmates with poor overall health have an increased susceptibility to disease.

Second, the Nation's 500,000 correctional employees—and the thousands of daily visitors to prisons and jails—may be exposed to disease unless appropriate precautions are taken. These employees and visitors in turn may infect family members and others in the community.

Third, inmates with communicable diseases who are released without having been effectively treated may transmit these conditions in the community, threatening public health.

Finally, the threat of releasing untreated inmates with contagious diseases involves more than the possibility of infecting other people in the community. Inmates who are released with untreated conditions—including communicable disease, chronic disease, and mental illness—may also become a serious financial burden on community health care systems. An illustration suggests the seriousness of this danger. Outbreaks of multidrug/resistant tuberculosis that have occurred in prisons have spread into the community as inmates with the disease have been released, resulting in deaths and enormous public costs to control the infection. Efforts to control the resurgence of tuberculosis in the early 1990s—fueled at least in part by released inmates—cost New York City alone more than $1 billion.

Growing Dangers and Costs

The danger and expense to the community of releasing untreated inmates are likely to grow for several reasons.

- Prison and jail populations are increasing. The number of inmates is growing about 5 percent per year and is now more than 1.9 million. Each week, the Nation must add more than 1,100 prison beds to keep up with the rapidly growing inmate population.

  "High rates of communicable disease . . . among . . . [inmates creates] a critical need for prevention, screening, and treatment services."

- Certain diseases are more common among substance abusers than among the rest of the population, including HIV/AIDS, hepatitis B and C, and tuberculosis. At the same time, an increasing proportion of inmates are substance abusers. In 1985, only 38,900—8.6 percent—of State prison

92

inmates were serving time for drug offenses as their most serious crime committed. By 1995, that number had increased almost sixfold to 224,900—22.7 percent of all inmates. This change has brought more individuals into the corrections system who are at very high risk for acquiring and transmitting HIV, hepatitis, and tuberculosis.

- Even though correctional populations are still younger than the national average, the Nation's prison and jail populations are aging. In 1997, almost 30 percent of inmates in State or Federal prisons were between the ages of 35 and 44, compared with 23 percent in 1991. The rise was offset by a decline in the percentage of inmates aged 18–34. (The percentage of inmates 55 years old or older did not change—about 3 percent in both years.) A similar phenomenon is occurring in jails. As the inmate population gets older, chronic diseases associated with increasing age, such as diabetes and hypertension, can be expected to increase among correctional populations.

Window of Opportunity

Prisons and jails offer uniquely important opportunities for improving disease control in the community by providing health care and disease prevention programs to a large and concentrated population of individuals at high risk for disease. Prisons and jails make it possible to reach a population that is largely underserved and difficult to identify and treat in the general community. Inmates often have little interaction with the health care system before and after being incarcerated.

> *"Prisons and jails offer uniquely important opportunities for improving disease control."*

Most inmates come from poor communities where health care services, other than hospital emergency rooms, are largely inaccessible or underutilized. For a variety of reasons, many inmates do not seek diagnosis or treatment for illness before arriving in prison or jail. Because inmates are literally a "captive" audience, it is vastly more efficient and effective to screen and treat them while incarcerated than to conduct extensive outreach in local communities designed to encourage at-risk individuals to go to a clinic for testing and treatment. By introducing routine prevention, screening, and treatment into prisons and jails, incarceration offers an opportunity for an underserved high-risk population to receive prevention and treatment services.

There is another important advantage to reaching this population while it is still incarcerated. Many illnesses that are prevalent among inmates are linked to a number of other health problems. There are high rates of coinfection with HIV/AIDS, sexually transmitted diseases, hepatitis B and C, and tuberculosis. Substance abusers are at very high risk for HIV, hepatitis, and other infectious and chronic diseases. Unless adequately treated, people with mental illness often "medicate" themselves with alcohol or illicit drugs. By preventing or treating one of the conditions these individuals suffer from, the development of several other conditions may be averted.

Finally, correctional facilities offer this population access to prevention and treatment services at a time when their thinking is less likely to be clouded by active drug use or by pressing survival concerns, such as the need for employment, housing, or food.

> *"The reduction in adverse health consequences to society that correctional agencies can achieve is . . . worth the cost."*

Most inmates have not had access to routine health care before being incarcerated. Correctional systems pay the consequences of this lack of preincarceration prevention and treatment. Because inmates may not have had eye examinations before they went to prison or jail that might have detected treatable incipient diabetes, the correctional system must pay for addressing the medical consequences of their untreated diabetes. Nevertheless, it is cost effective for correctional systems to implement proven approaches to preventing, screening for, and treating disease among inmates. The reduction in adverse health consequences to society that correctional agencies can achieve is unquestionably worth the cost of providing these services. Analyses . . . document that screening for syphilis and latent tuberculosis infection, and providing counseling and testing for HIV infection, will save more money in averted medical costs than would be needed to implement the interventions.

Surmountable Barriers

Corrections agencies can most effectively limit the number of untreated inmates they release into the community by addressing diseases that (1) are highly prevalent among inmates, (2) pose a serious threat to public health, and (3) can be effectively prevented or treated. On the one hand, these are the conditions that, if untreated, are most likely to spread in prisons and jails and to pose a threat to public health as inmates are released. On the other hand, these are the conditions that the correctional health care system is best equipped to prevent or treat.

Many correctional systems have experienced difficulties in attempting to improve their health care services for the most prevalent, serious, and preventable or treatable diseases and mental disorders among inmates. Correctional systems have faced the following barriers:

- *Leadership barriers.* Many administrators and other decisionmakers in correctional systems and in the community are not aware of the need or the opportunity to improve correctional health care, while others lack the political will or commitment to take the lead.
- *Logistical barriers.* The short stay of many jail inmates increases the challenge to identify quickly inmates with serious conditions, particularly communicable diseases.

- *Financial barriers.* Correctional administrators may feel they cannot provide adequate medical care for all inmates because other prison or jail services have a higher priority for the limited funds available.
- *Policy barriers.* Many correctional systems will not allow mentally ill inmates with substance abuse problems to participate in outpatient and residential drug treatment programs if they continue to use prescription medications to treat their mental disorders. . . .

The local community—in particular, local public health departments—contributes to the barriers correctional systems face in providing health care by not sharing responsibility for improving correctional health care services. . . . However, there are well-documented ways of overcoming these barriers through collaborations between correctional and public health agencies.

Chapter 3

Should Prisons Use Inmate Labor?

Prison Labor: An Overview

by Joseph T. Hallinan

About the author: *Joseph T. Hallinan is the author of* Going Up the River: Travels in a Prison Nation, *from which the following viewpoint is excerpted.*

At the Eastern Oregon Correctional Institution, a medium-security prison in the famous mill town of Pendleton, inmates don't make license plates anymore. They make money. Pretty good money, too: $6.25 an hour, on average.

For-Profit Factories

That's because the prison here, like prisons across America, is turning itself into a for-profit factory, cashing in on a tight labor market and public disenchantment with rehabilitation programs. In 1994, Oregon voters overwhelmingly approved an amendment to the state constitution known as Measure 17. For more than one hundred years, the state's inmate work program had existed primarily as a rehabilitative tool, designed to keep inmates busy and to teach them usable skills. No more: Measure 17 required that the work programs be run instead "to achieve a net profit."

So today the state's inmate work program is run as a for-profit business under an assumed business name, Inside Oregon Enterprises [IOE]. It functions, in essence, as a convict version of Kelly Girls [temporary employment agency], leasing inmates to companies in need of labor. Although the inmates must be paid market wages, employers offer no retirement, vacation, or health benefits; nor do they pay for Social Security, workers' compensation, or Medicare. Altogether, according to IOE, hiring inmates can cut an employer's payroll costs by 35 percent.

Among IOE's best-known employers is Prison Blues. It makes a line of clothing that features T-shirts, jackets, and jeans some of them identical to the ones worn by Oregon inmates. The company, which is owned by a businessman from Portland, employs one hundred inmates. Its 47,000-square-foot factory is located behind the walls of the prison in Pendleton. In addition to paying the inmates, Prison Blues also pays IOE a 6 percent royalty on its net sales.

Depending on the work Oregon's inmates perform, the state calculates that it can earn a profit of between seventy-six cents and $1.14 for every hour of their labor. The Oregon Department of Corrections expects that by 2006 it will make $10 million a year from its inmates. This prospect is so appealing that the state now plans to equip each new prison with built-in factory space.

The penchant for profit springs in many ways from the 1970s, when federal courts around the country began seizing control of state prisons. In many cases, federal judges ordered costly reforms, forcing previously tight-fisted corrections departments to go on shopping sprees. Perhaps the best example is the state of Texas. In 1980, when U.S. District Court Judge William Wayne Justice issued his written opinion in *Ruiz v. Estelle*, the state spent just $300 million on its prisons. In 1985, it spent $1 billion. . . .

From Golf Shirts to Travel Reservations

Profitability is contagious. Across the country, prisons began to seek more and more ways to raise money. Some, like those in Oregon, even turned themselves into profit-making corporations. As odd as this practice sounds, it is increasingly common. In South Carolina, not only are American corporations doing business behind bars, so are foreign ones. Among the most recent arrivals is Kwalu, Inc. In 1997, this furniture maker disassembled its plant in Capetown, South Africa, packed it into forty crates, and shipped it across the ocean to a prison in the tiny town of Ridgeland, population 1,071.

The move, says owner David Horwitz, has worked out "exceptionally well." The company employs nearly ninety inmates at an average wage of just more than $7 an hour. That is more than triple the wage Kwalu paid its South African workers. But the work ethic is so poor in South Africa, Horwitz says, that the greater efficiency of the inmates more than makes up for the higher labor cost. And in a state where growing employers worry constantly about finding skilled workers, Horwitz is smiling. "Nowhere else," he says, "can we double our labor force in a matter of a month."

Kwalu was recruited to South Carolina by Tony Ellis, the state's director of prison industries. "They were actually looking to buy land in Florida," Ellis says when I ask him how Kwalu ended up in South Carolina. "And I said, 'Come on up here. I can assure you of a labor force.'" On top of that, he says, "We put 'em up in a thirty-seven-thousand-square-foot building down there."

> *"The Oregon Department of Corrections expects that by 2006 it will make $10 million a year from [inmate labor]."*

Like many prison-industry programs, the one in South Carolina is self-sustaining. It gets no state funds. Companies like Kwalu pay inmates' wages through the industries program, which keeps a percentage of the payment as its fee. Most years, says Ellis, the program breaks even or makes a slight profit.

Annual revenues exceed $18 million, "and we plow that money right back into the program."

But it's still a tough business, marked by high turnover, fickle employers, and international competition. South Carolina's inmates used to make golf shirts, Ellis says, but lost that contract when the company moved production to Mexico. Inmates at one of the women's prisons used to make lingerie for Victoria's Secret, but they lost that contract, too. Now, instead of underwear, the women make travel reservations. "You'll call Omega World Travel, you know, and they'll hit a switch and kick the work down to us," Ellis says. Inmates aren't allowed access to the traveler's credit card information. When it comes time to pay for a ticket, the call is transferred to a civilian employee.

A New Era

Some, including Morgan Reynolds, see programs like the one in South Carolina as just the beginning of a new era of prison for profit. Reynolds is an economics professor at Texas A&M University, and he directs the criminal justice programs at the National Center for Policy Analysis. The center is a conservative advocacy group from Dallas that does not, Reynolds tells me, "make any pretense to be grassroots." It is funded not by government grants or do-good organizations, but by wealthy individuals who arguably would benefit from an increased use of inmate labor.

Classic prison jobs like making license plates, Reynolds says, are just part of a "tired old socialist model" of prison labor. In his new world, wardens are "marketers of prison labor" and prisons themselves are little more than industrial parks with bars. They should be built not where the crime is but where the jobs are. In Texas, he says, prisons could even take advantage of the North American Free Trade Agreement by making products near the border for shipment to Mexico. "You could put a prison between Houston and north of the border—McAllen, Brownsville—and create value-added there." Prisons, I think to myself, have created many things, but never value.

In the past, Reynolds tells me, prison administrators had been blind to the commercial opportunities of their institutions. But those opportunities now hold the key to their success. "It's pretty clear," he says, "that's where the future is if we're going to grow our prison population."

It was a chilling thought: the decision to consciously "grow" prisons, as if they were any other industry. But with the nation's unemployment rate at thirty-year lows [in the late 1990s], it was not entirely far-fetched. Businessmen now all but beg for prison labor. Among the most outspoken is Edwin Meese III, who served as attorney general during the Reagan administration. Meese is now chairman of the Enterprise Prison Institute, a for-profit group in McLean, Virginia, that is pushing for greater access to prison labor. As attorney general, Meese oversaw stiffened sentencing for drug offenses, which in turn swelled the nation's prisons. Now, on the lecture circuit, he totes a circuit board built by an inmate in a California prison, and speaks to business groups of the potential for the nation's inmates. . . .

[Since the 1920s] it has been a violation of federal law for state prisons to sell their products in interstate commerce—unless, like the programs in South Carolina and Oregon, they are certified by a federal program known as Prison Industry Enhancement, or PIE. The PIE program was created in 1979, and until recently has been all but dormant. In 1998, for instance, thirty-five states were certified to participate in the program, but, all told, they employed just twenty-six hundred inmates, or about two tenths of 1 percent of the nation's state prison population.

> *"Wardens [have become] 'marketers of prison labor' and prisons themselves are little more than industrial parks with bars."*

Under the provisions of PIE, inmates must be paid the same wages as free workers engaged in similar work. They must also be allowed to keep at least 20 percent of what they earn. The rest of their wages can be withheld to pay income taxes, child support obligations, room and board charges, and payments due to victim assistance funds.

Although some of the inmates employed through PIE do sophisticated work (Oregon inmates, for instance, turn paper maps into digitized ones), the vast majority perform menial labor. . . .

Filling a Niche

For months, says Julie Glessner, whose family owns Boomsma [a chicken farm in Clarion, Iowa], she ran ads in the newspaper looking for help, and for months she got virtually no replies. Desperate, she applied to the Iowa Department of Labor for permission to import workers from Mexico. The department told her to try the prison first.

Today, twenty-three of the farm's thirty daily employees are inmates. They sort, clean, and package 1.3 million eggs a day, 7 days a week, 365 days a year, including Christmas. The inmates, all minimum-security prisoners convicted of nonviolent offenses, are supervised by one guard. He is armed not with a gun but with a cell phone.

"It's not as bad as I thought," says Ricardo Herrera, a thirty-two-year-old inmate serving a "double nickel"—two five-year terms for drunk driving and delivery of marijuana. Herrera is from Calexico, California, where he has two kids, a six-year-old boy and a four-year-old girl. He came to Iowa in 1989 to work at a slaughterhouse run by Iowa Beef Processors, the meatpacking giant of the Midwest. One night, he says, the cops pulled him over and found marijuana in his car, and that's how he ended up here.

Herrera spends his entire workday pushing a broom inside a plywood henhouse, cleaning up the feathers and manure produced by 100,000 Hyline chickens. . . .

For this he is paid $6 an hour. After taxes and other required deductions, he gets to keep $1.20. "It's a little dusty and dirty," he says, "but I don't see anything wrong with it."

But Mark Smith, the union president, does. Jobs like Herrera's, he says, do little more than provide subsidies for businesspeople like the Glessners. "Maybe this is cynical," he tells me. "But I believe they need a source of cheap and compliant labor." Besides, he says, "You tell me how shoveling chicken shit at Boomsma's is going to prepare you to go to work. It just doesn't make sense. If Boomsma's says they can't find labor—hell, no, not at six dollars an hour. So they go to the prison."

The Iowa program is run by Roger Baysden, a forty-nine-year-old retired food broker who believes fervently in the rehabilitative power of work. "There's only two things that'll change an inmate," he tells me, "and that's work and God. I gotta count on God to do his stuff, and I'll take care of the work." Until he joined the program in 1997, Baysden had never been in a prison. He was surprised to learn that 40 percent of the state's inmates would return to prison one day, and even more surprised to learn that the prison system did little to improve those odds.

"In Iowa, when they get out of prison, they get a hundred-dollar bill and a one-way bus ticket," he says. "Now, what are you going to do with a one-way bus ticket and a hundred-dollar bill?"

Like all states, Iowa requires inmates to work. One of the lingering myths about prison is that inmates are allowed to loaf. The average workday in prison varies between 6.5 and 7.4 hours—a full day after deducting the time spent moving inmates to and from their cells, feeding them, and counting them. But in many cases, prison work is make-work. "You can only mop a floor so many times," says Baysden. And besides, such jobs offer little prospect for earning a living wage in the outside world.

Job Placement or Unfair Competition?

So the state decided to try something different, and in 1995 it renewed efforts to place its inmates in private industry. So far, the program has had limited success. Of the state's 6,900 inmates, only 200 work for private businesses. But Baysden expects that the number will soon top 300. The inmates make between $5.25 and $10 an hour. Of this, they get to keep the requisite 20 percent. To participate in the program, inmates must meet three requirements:
- They cannot have been charged with a crime against another person.
- They must have a clean prison disciplinary record.
- They must have a scheduled release date.

To avoid having the inmates exploited, Baysden says, he also requires every contractor of prison labor to offer a job to an inmate upon his release. So far, says Baysden, they've placed nineteen inmates in full-time jobs, "and that's a pretty good record."

David A. Smith, director of the public policy department of the AFL-CIO, disagrees: "This is coerced, incarcerated labor competing in a commercial marketplace against free workers." To him, using prison labor in America is no different from using prison labor in China.

But inmates see it differently. "Ain't no comparison," says Dick Williams, a forty-six-year-old inmate with a silver front tooth and a golden voice. "This is not forced. This is the premier place to be." "This," in his case, is a small room on the second floor of the North Central Correctional Facility, a minimum-security prison sixty miles southwest of Julie Glessner's egg farm. Here Williams works as a telemarketer for the Heartland Communications Group, a publisher based in Fort Dodge, Iowa.

> *"[To one critic] using prison labor in America is no different from using prison labor in China."*

He spends eight hours a day with fifteen or so other convicts, each of them hunkered down in a cubicle trying to sell magazine subscriptions or services of one sort or another. Across the room from him a pedophile pushes the Iowa Political Hotline. A few cubicles over, another inmate makes appointments for salesmen from Pet Alert of the Carolinas, which sells shock collars for dogs. ("Good evening, I'm representing Pet Alert of the Carolinas. . . .")

Williams's specialty is farmers. He starts dialing at 7 A.M., before the farmers are in the fields. He tries to get them to advertise their used tractors and other items in Farmers Hot Line Iowa. He's been at it fifteen months, he said, and loves his job.

The inmate work program at North Central has proved so popular that the county has built an industrial park next to the prison. Inmates can walk through the back gate of the prison and into the park, which is actually a warehouse about the size of a football field. Inside, the warehouse is divided into half a dozen small, wall-less shops, although "shops" is a bit grandiose. One inmate, wearing a Walkman, sits alone at a card table. On his left is an electric skillet filled with water; on his right, a pair of tongs. In front of him is a stack of raw rubber gaskets for vacuum cleaners. His job is to vulcanize the rubber, which he does by plopping a gasket into the boiling water of the skillet for a few seconds, then plucking it out with the tongs. Plop. Pluck. All day long. Eight hours a day.

Developing Work Habits

It was not, I imagined, the kind of work that would lead to a better life. But I was wrong about that. My last stop in Iowa was at the Diamond Crystal Foods plant in Bondurant, just a few hundred yards from the women's prison. Diamond Crystal is a packager of dry blended food products, and the work here is not a lot more challenging than vulcanizing gaskets. Basically, workers tend machines that take bulk containers of products like Kool-Aid and dry pudding mix and seal them into tidy six-ounce packages. Diamond Crystal runs two shifts a day and employs 130 people. Inmates account for twelve of those employees, or a little less than 10 percent of the workforce. Guards bring the women down from the prison in a van every morning, says Chuck House, the plant manager. "Then in the afternoon they bring the fresh people down."

Like every employer I talked to, he loved his inmates. "One nice thing about them," he says, "is they don't mind working overtime. Some of our people, you say, 'Overtime.' They say, 'Overtime? What, you want me to work overtime?' These people, 'Oh, yeah, you betcha.'"

The women wear prison garb while at the plant—blue pants and a chambray shirt with DOC stenciled on the back—and guards make unannounced inspections twice each shift. Inmates are not allowed to fraternize with the other workers. If they get too friendly—a suggestive pat on the back, anything like that—they are bounced back to the prison. But other than that, says House, "We treat them exactly like we treat anybody else, including the pay scale and the insurance plan."

So far, he says, there have been few problems. Diamond Crystal has been involved in the program for two years, and over that time it has hired half a dozen women after their parole from the prison. One of them is Karen Smith, who is forty-five and has served sixteen months for passing bad checks. Those were hard times for her, she said, because she missed more than a year in the life of her daughter, now seventeen. She's been out of prison for a year and a half now, and has been employed at Diamond Crystal the entire time. "This is the longest job I've ever stayed at," she says.

Before Diamond Crystal, her previous prison job had been on a community work crew, sprucing up golf courses and other public grounds. It paid $3.50 a day. The first day on the job at Diamond Crystal she earned $7.70 an hour. This enabled her to save enough money—$1,800—to get a new apartment, a second-hand car, and a new start on life.

People in the free world, she says, don't understand how precious a nest egg is to someone like her. Without it, she would have left prison with only $100 and the bus ticket that is supposed to provide a one-way trip. "When you come out and you don't have anything," she says, "those old ways start to come back."

This seemed so obviously and fundamentally true that I began to wonder why every state did not employ a program like Iowa's; why every able inmate was not doing a job that would help keep those old ways at bay.

Iowa's motivations, I knew, were not purely altruistic. It did not embark on the PIE program because its citizens were particularly kind or smart or beneficent. Iowa's employers simply needed workers. Unemployment was at a thirty-year low, and inmates were suddenly valuable. But this situation would not last forever. One day unemployment would creep back up, and law-abiding people would again need work. I asked Roger Baysden what would happen then, and he said that the program would probably be curtailed or even eliminated. It was then, I thought, that the old ways would start to come back.

Prison Labor Teaches Valuable Job Skills

by Morgan Reynolds and Knut Rostad

About the authors: *Morgan Reynolds is director of the Criminal Justice Center at the National Center for Policy Analysis. Knut Rostad is president of the Enterprise Prison Institute, an organization that encourages American companies to use prison labor.*

The Bush administration has announced its intention to reach across party lines and look at old problems in new ways. Perhaps nowhere would this strategy reap a greater harvest than in jointly alleviating the 93 percent unemployment rate behind the gates of American prisons and a workforce shortage that threatens American competitiveness.

The Skilled Worker Shortage

This year [2001] more than 600,000 convicts will be released from prisons into our towns and neighborhoods—most released on parole.

- Only 9 percent of these inmates have had full-time vocational training or education programs while in prison, and fewer still gained any real work experience.
- In a typical state prison, only 7 percent of inmates work in jobs producing goods and services for use beyond prison fences.

In the face of these facts, it is not surprising that many end up in prison again. Almost two-thirds of those released in any year will be rearrested—and a majority of those will be returned to prison—within three years. . . . [According to the Bureau of Justice Statistics], only 50 percent of parolees successfully completed their parole in 1990, and by 1999 the figure had shrunk to 43 percent. For these dismal results, taxpayers pay $40 billion a year to fund our nation's jails and prisons.

The irony of the "high unemployment/recidivism" syndrome is that it coexists with a workforce crisis. American business faces tremendous hurdles filling jobs at all levels with qualified American workers. The National Association of Manufacturers [NAM] says that a "skills gap threatens U.S. competitiveness," a gap that often involves poor work habits like workers failing to "get to work on time and stay for a full day."

The NAM is not alone in its assessment. *Fortune* magazine reports that the National Tooling and Machining Association estimates 25,000 jobs are going unfilled and concludes, "There's nobody left to hire, at least nobody with rudimentary skills who understands it's necessary to show up on time every day." David Goodreau, president of the Burbank, California-based Newman Machine Works, adds, "Today, many manufacturers are crippled from a dearth of skilled, motivated and reliable workers with an aptitude for math and a sense of teamwork. Too often we are left with unskilled, lower-wage workers who just aren't world-class workers."

Offshore operation is the most common structural answer to the domestic skills gap for manufacturing and service companies alike. Mexico has become the "New South" for many North American manufacturers seeking a productive, close-by workforce, and as the Internet and information economy take hold, the new workforce may be more far-flung. MIT [Massachusetts Institute of Technology] professor Michael Dertouzos sees white-collar "back-office" functions now heading to India from North America and Europe and predicts the number will rise over the next decade to as many as 50 million jobs, paying on average $20,000 a year (in 1999 dollars).

The Benefits of Prison Manufacturing

There are, of course, alternatives to India for American companies. For labor-intensive manufacturing, assembly or service companies that might head offshore, what might be called an "InPrison" operation can provide an excellent, cost-effective domestic alternative. Experience and research reveal that business managers find inmates surprisingly motivated, reliable and productive. How productive?

A Deloitte & Touche [corporate consulting firm] study in 1999 analyzed the unit labor costs and productivity of InPrison manufacturing settings and concluded that using inmates in tasks with a relatively short learning curve results in "greater than standard productivity" and "direct labor cost savings." A survey by the Enterprise Prison Institute [prison labor advocacy group] of InPrison business operations in Washington state revealed employers believe the single most valuable aspect of prison production is "the flexibility, reliability, and/or quality of the inmate labor."

> *"Using [inmate labor] . . . results in 'greater than standard productivity' and 'direct labor cost savings.'"*

Legislators and manufacturers alike who want a "world class" workforce might note the example of "Barbara Alvarado" (not her real name). Today, Barbara works as a quality assurance manager in Silicon Valley [near San Francisco, California]. She gained this position despite an employment history limited to selling used cars—until she went to prison. Barbara completed two years of work for Joint Venture Electronics [JVE] while serving her prison term for a drug offense at the Central California Women's Facility.

> *"Prisoners gain work skills . . . while industry alleviates its workforce crisis."*

Under the watchful eye of industry veteran Jack Lee, Barbara was trained in every aspect of printed circuit board harness and cable assembly in a training program based on high-quality military standards.

"Our company orientation revolves around training," Lee explains. "We cross-train employees in all operations in order to be as flexible as possible. While I set production requirements, scheduling and staffing decisions are made by departmental group leaders in conjunction with other leaders. By the time an employee leaves us they will have a well-rounded knowledge in electronics specifically, and production supervision management generally." Thirty-three women who worked for JVE have been paroled and have kept in contact over the past four years. About half work in electronics or management, and one—just one—has been returned to prison. This compares to a statewide recidivism rate of 50 percent.

Future Goals

What can the [Bush] administration do to both cut prison unemployment and alleviate the workforce crisis in the economy? Leadership should occupy the middle ground among the conflicting interests surrounding prison labor policy and attract broad, bipartisan support. Goals would include:

- Supplement traditional government-run prison industries like apparel manufacturing with private businesses that employ inmates in technologically driven jobs.
- Eliminate the requirement that government agencies purchase prison-made goods.
- Encourage partnership, contracts and outsourcing in order to recruit private sector companies for prison production.
- Encourage faith-based organizations to provide comprehensive programs for inmate training, jobs and mentoring.
- Monitor the transition to insure net job additions as new enterprises replace "old economy" prison jobs.

The administration also should coordinate the efforts of agencies like the Department of Health and Human Services and the Department of Labor, along with private efforts, to improve and expand the training and employing of prison inmates by private companies and nonprofits. The overall idea is to make prison labor available to American industry on terms similar to those of the general marketplace. In the process, prisoners gain work skills and raise the chances of lowering their recidivism rates after release, while industry alleviates its workforce crisis.

Former Attorney General Edwin Meese often speaks about how little prison management has changed over the decades. Meanwhile, technological and political changes sweeping the world economy have upended the former Soviet Union, drastically altered the economy of China and reengineered the business models of the world's greatest corporations. It is time for these same ideas and forces to change prisons as we know them—to make free market production and wages as common and important inside prison as outside. The new administration should make prisons over.

Prison Labor Reduces Incarceration Costs

by Robert D. Atkinson

About the author: *Robert D. Atkinson is vice president of the Progressive Policy Institute, a nonpartisan political research organization.*

Prison labor has two main benefits. First, it reduces inmate recidivism, thereby reducing crime and lowering prison costs. Second, if done right, it produces "profits" which can be used to offset the taxpayer-financed costs of incarcerating prisoners.

Improved Employment Prospects

Studies have shown that inmates who work in prison industries or had vocational training have better outcomes when they are released from prison. Research suggests that the failure of ex-offenders to maintain employment may contribute to high recidivism rates. In 1991, the Federal Bureau of Prisons released an analysis of the Post Release Employment Project. More than 7,000 program participants were evaluated over a two-year period. The study found that those offenders who received training and work experience while in prison had fewer conduct problems and were less likely to be arrested the first year after release. In 1993, the New York State Department of Correctional Services conducted a study of release outcomes for offenders employed in the production of eyeglasses, which found that the vocational program was effective in lowering rates of probation failure and rearrest for program participants. At 12 months after release, 3 percent of program participants had been returned to department custody compared to 11 percent of the control group; and at 84 months after release, 34 percent of program participants had been returned to department custody compared to 54 percent of the control group. An FPI [Federal Prison Industries] study found that upon release from prison, workers were 24 percent more likely to obtain a full-time or day-labor jobs during this time. Moreover, by the end of the first year of release, 10.1 percent of the comparison group inmates had been rearrested or had their conditional release revoked, compared with 6.6 percent of program participants. Further, 72 percent of program participants found and maintained employment during this period, compared with just 63 percent of comparison group inmates. The study concludes:

> It appears that prison employment in an industrial work setting and vocational or apprenticeship training can have both short and long term effects that reduce the likelihood of recidivism, particularly for men. . . . Therefore, correctional industries' work and training programs could help to reduce prison populations.

These studies are not surprising since statistics show that offenders are more likely to be unemployed at time of arrest. One study by the National Institute of Corrections found that up to 40 percent of all offenders were unemployed or marginally employed prior to arrest. A New York State Department of Labor study found that 83 percent of probation and parole violators were unemployed at the time of violation. Lower rates of recidivism are not just good for society by reducing crime, but also help keep prison populations smaller than they would otherwise be, saving taxpayers money.

Economic Benefits

Prison labor can also help offset the costs of housing prisoners, reducing taxpayer-financed costs while increasing GDP [gross domestic product]. When viewed from a growth economics perspective where the goal is to maximize national productivity and the output of goods and services, prison labor is a very good thing for the economy. The key to understanding this is to recognize that as new workers begin producing output, existing workers are not displaced permanently. They get jobs again and produce goods and services. In this case, the economy is better off because both civilian and prison workers are producing output. Supply creates its own demand. As these prison workers create output, a portion of the money returns to them and they consume items while in prison. But most of the money goes to reducing the costs of housing convicts, which in turn either allows taxes to be reduced or is used by the government to increase spending on other needed services. Either case raises demand for goods and services. In the case of tax cuts, consumers spend the money on goods and services. In the case of government expenditures, the government spends it on government services. Even if the companies pay less than minimum wage (which PPI [Progressive Policy Institute] opposes), the economy still benefits since the products sold will be cheaper, allowing consumers to spend their savings on other goods and services. In all these cases, when prisoners work, the economy is richer because more people are working. It is pretty simple. In the moderate term, employing prisoners doesn't raise unemployment but adds to the overall GDP.

> *"Prison labor can also help offset the costs of housing prisoners, reducing taxpayer-financed costs."*

Although some opponents might be willing to grant that in the moderate term employing prisoners is good for the economy, they might argue that the economy can't absorb new prisoners and that it will boost unemployment rates. Considering that seven million welfare recipients moved from welfare to work between 1996 and 2000 as the unemployment rate went down, it is clear that the economy can easily add several hundred thousand prisoners to the labor force over the next five years without increasing unemployment rates. In fact, as the experience of the late 1990s showed, increases in the labor force have no effect on the unemployment rate because new workers don't just work, they also become consumers.

Opposition to Prison Labor

In spite of the significant advantages of prison labor to both society and inmates, there are two main factors motivating its opponents: concern that making prisoners work is exploitative and fear that it will displace civilian business and labor. Both concerns stimulated the initial restrictions on prison labor put in place at the beginning of the 20th century and are motivating legislative efforts in Congress and the states to restrict it today.

To this day, the image most people have of prison labor comes from movies like "Cool Hand Luke," where workers are exploited by a sadistic foreman as they cut brush by the side of the road or break big rocks into small rocks. As a result of the vestiges of these images, some people reflexively oppose prison labor because they fear a return of such exploitation. Liberals in particular are prone to see prison labor as benefitting some vast "prison industrial complex" while exploiting an oppressed proletariat who have been unfairly imprisoned. For example, one University of Massachusetts website devoted to prisoner rights wrote:

> Convicted kidnapper Dino Navarrete doesn't smile much as he surveys the sewing machines at Soledad prison's sprawling workshop. The short, stocky man with tattoos rippling his muscles forearms earns 45 cents an hour making blue work shirts in a medium security prison near Monterey, California. After deductions, he earns about $60 for an entire month of nine hour days. "You know they're making money. Where's the money going to? It ain't going to us."

A [1999] article in the liberal journal, *American Prospect*, by University of Oregon professor Gordon Lafer decried the unfairness of prison labor, stating: "Prison workers can be hired, fired, or reassigned at will. Not only do they have no right to organize or strike; they also have no means of filing a grievance or voicing any kind of complaint whatsoever. They have no right to circulate an employee petition or newsletter, no right to call a meeting, and no access to the press." He complained that inmates are exploited because they get "no health insurance, no unemployment insurance, no vacation time." Lafer goes on to state that "prison labor is analogous to slave labor." He, like most liberal opponents, seems to miss the fundamental point: These are criminals who are serving time in prison for illegal activity and, as such, are deprived of some of the rights free people enjoy. Prisoners don't get vacations, that's why they are in prison.

No Exploitation

Moreover, the reality is that prison labor looks like normal labor; workers sewing garments, building furniture, recycling computers, answering phones, etc. The prison work environment is usually safer than the rest of the prison. In many cases, workers volunteer for work, because it is a lot more interesting and financially rewarding than watching TV all day. And, at least in the case of private work in prisons, work sites are subject to OSHA [Occupational Safety and Health Administration] inspections.

Notwithstanding this, many on the left feel that prisoners are often incarcerated unjustly (they either didn't really commit a crime, or they should not have been imprisoned for it) and as such, are victims of an oppressive state and profit-hungry corporations seeking to exploit their cheap labor. Many argue against prison labor on the grounds that we should do more to help the unemployed get jobs before they go to prison. Former Secretary of Labor Robert Reich states: "In other words, without really intending to do so, the nation is in the process of creating a giant jobs program for people who are likely to be unemployed. The only problem is, in order to be eligible for it, you've got to be in prison." Reich incorrectly assumes that prison labor is a substitute for civilian labor.

> *"The [U.S.] economy can easily add several hundred thousand prisoners to the labor force . . . without increasing unemployment."*

Finally, some on the left fear that if prison labor is expanded somehow there will be a greater incentive on the part of the state to put more people in prison through things like mandatory sentencing laws. In his campaign to end prison labor, Lafer concludes:

> Ultimately such stopgap measures [such as requiring prisoners to be paid prevailing wages] will be neither effective nor politically viable as long as correctional facilities continue to operate under the fiscal constraints imposed by mandatory sentencing laws. Building a consensus not only against the extensive employment of prisoners but also against mandatory sentencing laws will be a slow and arduous process, but we must undertake it if we hope to stop the expansion of prison labor before it gets much further. A "free market" economy ought to have no place for a vast army of prisoners undermining the wages of working people.

The reality is that there is no causal link between prison labor and higher incarceration. But Lafer and his fellow travelers essentially want fewer people put in prison so there will be less competition for civilian workers.

Taking Jobs from Civilians?

The second source of opposition stems from the fear that prison labor takes away jobs and business from civilian labor and businesses. Unions, businesses, and trade organizations have launched campaigns in the states and Congress to limit its expansion and even roll it back. They make the case that prison labor, especially as operated by FPI, is essentially unfair because it takes jobs from law abiding Americans and business from entrepreneurs. Opposition from businesses who lose contracts (and their conservative political supporters) is understandable. The fact that they are losing business to a government enterprise that employs prisoners at rock-bottom wages makes it doubly difficult for them to swallow. Likewise, workers who lose their jobs due to competition with prison labor feel particularly aggrieved.

Market displacement, however, doesn't mean that prison labor is not good for the nation nor that its benefits don't outweigh the costs. In fact, in many ways this debate is similar to the trade debate. While the evidence is clear that free trade helps grow the economy, it also hurts certain workers and firms in the short run. The same can be true with prison labor if the inmates are producing items that take work away from private companies (although prison labor has the advantage over trade in that it also results in more Americans working, whereas trade only changes the nature of the work, not the number of people working). The answer is to expand assistance for displaced workers and affected firms, not to stop prison labor.

One reason why opponents see prison labor as a zero-sum game that takes jobs from others is that their model of the economy is one in which there is a fixed amount of demand for goods and services. This fixed demand determines the number of jobs and amount of business. If another business fills the demand, the companies and workers originally fulfilling it will cut back on output and the economy will be no better off. Lafer states: "Prison labor must be opposed on the more durable basis that it threatens free labor."

According to Lafer, making prisoners work real jobs (making car parts, taking airline reservations, sewing shirts, etc.) as opposed to "carrying boulders from one side of the road to another . . . takes jobs away from people on the outside" and is "at its heart anti labor." Labor is not alone, as businesses wave the small-business flag to argue that prison labor takes from civilian business to support prison business. If there were a limited and immutable demand for auto parts, airline reservations, and shirts, then substituting prison labor for civilian labor would simply transfer jobs from one group of Americans to another with no net benefit. But, as discussed above, it is not as if resources laid off in the private sector remain dormant in perpetuity. The capital, labor, and entrepreneurial talents will be redeployed and produce wealth and income.

> *"When prisoners work, the economy is better off."*

Idle Prisoners Are the Wrong Prescription

There is no doubt that in some cases prison labor, especially when conducted by prison enterprises like FPI, can result in companies losing contracts and some of their workers losing jobs. For example, in 1998, Glamour Glove, a Long Island, N.Y., maker of gloves, was in jeopardy of losing a portion of its government contracting when FPI decided to invest prison labor in glove manufacuring. Through legislative pressure, Glamour Glove was able to prevent this. In these cases, it is important to provide assistance to the workers and allow companies to make the adjustment, just as we do with companies negatively impacted by trade. But even if Glamour Glove or other companies were to lose their contracts, it is important to recognize that prison labor isn't simply a zero-sum game—it adds to overall economic output. As a result, when viewed from this growth economics perspective, it is clear that the opposition's prescription to keep these prison workers idle or, even worse, have them break rocks, does nothing to add to the economic output and wealth of our economy. When prisoners work, the economy is better off. The total economic output of society is larger than what it would be if those prisoners were just moving rocks.

The majority of Americans support prison labor because they believe that prisoners should help offset some of the costs of incarceration. It costs approximately $40 billion annually to incarcerate prisoners in local, state, and federal prisons. That works out to approximately $20,000 a year per prisoner. Surely prisoners can work and contribute something to help pay for this so taxpayers don't have to spend as much. Opponents of prison labor use the fact that some prison laborers are incarcerated for life with no chance of release to argue that the focus on reduced recidivism is a sham. The fact is that requiring a life-inmate to work and contribute a portion of his/her pay to room and board is consistent with the notion of the prisoner's responsibility to give something back to society as payment for his/her crimes. . . .

There is a lot that can and should be done to ensure that workers and businesses benefit in the New Economy. Opposing prison labor is not one of them. In fact, limiting prison labor would lower economic growth, while reducing the effectiveness of prisons to move prisoners to productive and law-abiding lives when they are released.

Prison Labor Facilitates Inmate Rehabilitation

by Bob Wignall

About the author: *Bob Wignall is a training manager for Prison Rehabilitative Industries and Diversified Enterprises (PRIDE), which provides job-skills training to inmates.*

Mike has just arrived at the Greyhound station in Tampa, Florida. He carries a plastic bag with his belongings. His clothing appears new and somewhat uncomfortable, but adequate and clean. He seems nervous, as it is apparent that the bus stop's noise and activity confuse him. He views the scene as if it is a foreign land. After looking and walking around for several minutes, he locates a telephone booth and calls a person he has never met. This call is critical, as it will contribute significantly to whether the man returns to where he came from—one of Florida's state prisons.

Rehabilitation and Reintegration Through Job Training

With 600,000 inmates released annually from federal and state prisons—23,000 in Florida alone—arrivals of newly released men and women at bus stations with less than $100 in cash and no wallet, state identification, driver's license nor outside support are frequent around the nation. At this point, the ex-offender is perhaps most vulnerable to external factors that may lead to rearrest, reconviction and re-incarceration. If a process can be designed to facilitate offenders' transition and reintegration into the community by assisting and supporting them immediately after their release and until they are stabilized in the community, their chances for success are greatly increased. With recidivism rates for state inmates estimated at between 40 percent and 70 percent, it is essential to support ex-offenders and help them work through the difficulties they will encounter finding and keeping jobs.

In Florida, the nonprofit company operating prison industries is Prison Rehabilitative Industries and Diversified Enterprises (PRIDE). PRIDE's Re-Entry model serves to address its mission—to reduce recidivism by providing job skills training for inmates while incarcerated, as well as post-release job placement. The concept, proved over time, adheres to a process of inmate rehabilitation beginning with the first day of work in a PRIDE industry and ending when ex-offenders successfully find and sustain jobs through community reintegration, which can take up to one year.

Mike's call is made to Labor Line Services, the toll-free, 24-hour transition and job placement company associated with PRIDE. After speaking with a transition coordinator, Mike is directed to a shelter for the night and provided with job leads. He may be given a clothing voucher, funds for housing and money to buy a bicycle, work boots or other similar essentials. He will be instructed to apply for a driver's license or, at a minimum, a state identification card. If he has special needs, he may be referred to drug and alcohol counseling, a local job service agency or other similar support networks.

> *"Recidivism [can be reduced] by providing job skills training for inmates while incarcerated."*

The transition coordinator understands that the ex-offender must be placed into a position as soon as possible, therefore, the objective is to complete the placement within 48 hours of the ex-offender's arrival in Tampa. The seriousness of the situation is recognized and intense, and extensive efforts are generated. This man may be part of the 86 percent of former PRIDE prison industry workers who are placed after leaving state prison. But he could just as easily be part of the 14 percent who are reincarcerated. The gap between these two groups, in many cases, is not wide and without the right counseling and support, the man may join that vast group of ex-offenders who are returned to Department of Correction (DOC) control.

PRIDE and Prison Industry

Since 1981, PRIDE has been operating prison industries in Florida's state prisons as a nonprofit corporation, independent of, but in cooperation with, the Florida DOC, and serves to complement other vocational and educational programs offered in Florida state prisons. Three equally important PRIDE missions are: to support security by reducing idleness and providing incentives for good behavior, reduce state government costs by using inmate labor to produce goods and services that do not seek to unreasonably compete with private sector firms, and enhance inmate rehabilitative goals by closely duplicating the operating activities of free-world companies. As in other states, correctional industry managers and supervisors in Florida understand the importance of training their work force, changing anti-social behaviors, instilling the work ethic and offsetting the dependency inherent in the prison environment to enhance inmates' chances at success once released.

Approximately 5,000 inmates, male and female, work annually in PRIDE's 55 industries located in 20 Florida state prisons. Industries include traditional license plate and furniture manufacturing and textile operations, as well as sophisticated industries, such as denture, optical and print industries. Producing 3,000 products, PRIDE's 2000 annual sales exceeded $95 million. Of the 500 PRIDE inmates released each year, PRIDE has been consistently successful in achieving its goals: to place 75 percent of inmates in jobs upon release, many in positions related to their industry training.

One of the most touted benefits of traditional prison industry is its social mission—rehabilitation. The fundamental objective of prison labor is to transform unskilled, untrained, uneducated inmates who lack the most basic social skills into productive workers according to free-world standards. The prison industry training program succeeds through the time-tested on-the-job training (OJT) philosophy, in which inmates are placed in industrial programs with precise, detailed and increasingly more demanding job tasks. In PRIDE's *Inmate Program Handbook*, provided to each inmate worker during his or her orientation to industry work, the social mission can clearly be seen:

> PRIDE conducts certified OJT programs that give inmate workers the opportunity to learn new skills and work habits. OJT is the process of teaching work skills through demonstration, instruction and practice in an actual work setting. PRIDE's OJT provides offenders with meaningful work during incarceration and the skills necessary to find and keep good jobs after release. PRIDE training is formal, structured and certified to meet private sector industry or state vocational training standards.

Start and End with PRIDE

Charged by the Florida Legislature to operate prison industries and to perform post-release transition assistance and job placement, PRIDE integrates formal job training and job placement components, recognizing that its mission continues after inmates are released from prison. To better define the PRIDE program and its priorities, the Florida Legislature passed the 60/40 statute in 1996, requiring PRIDE to maintain a work force of not fewer than 60 percent of its inmates with sentences of 10 years or shorter. The perception by some legislators is that industries may choose to hire inmates with longer sentences to reduce the traditionally high prison industry turnover rates that vary from 50 percent to 150 percent annually. The statute places the industry rehabilitation focus on the shorter-term inmates (and the resulting higher turnover and training costs) rather than on the purely business concerns, which perhaps are better met by longer-term inmates.

PRIDE has been able to balance the requirement for self-sufficiency as it receives no subsidies from the state and traditionally returns money to the state to pay for incarceration costs and the high training and post-release costs, leading to lower recidivism rates. This is achieved through a comprehensive job training and community placement program that seeks to offer ex-offenders a seamless transition from PRIDE support within the wire to support upon release.

The benefits of working in a structured correctional industry environment may be lost to the ex-offender if a similarly structured routine is not in place for the ex-offender upon release. Job placement assistance is a benefit resulting from the ex-offender's time spent successfully in one of PRIDE's prison industries that qualifies him or her for in-depth pre- and post-release assistance. By the end of a sentence, the ex-inmate has completed several components of a process designed to help achieve success after release. The process begins the first day the inmate worker is on the PRIDE payroll, as the program model emphasizes the placement component from day one.

On-the-Job Training

After an inmate worker has completed an employment application at one of PRIDE's industries and has been approved for hiring by the industry manager, based on industry needs, educational level and remainder of sentence, he or she receives an *Inmate Program Handbook* during the initial orientation. The handbook outlines the OJT program, which lasts approximately nine months; inmate compensation; victim restitution; assistance with parole and clemency release; correspondence course funding; and new hire, employability skills and self-development workshops. Equally important to the new inmate worker is the section on prerelease workshops and the post-release job placement program. Inmates learn from the beginning that if they start and end with PRIDE, they will receive assistance while in prison and upon release.

The industry manager will place the inmate in one of 300 certified training programs, 500 to 4,000 hours in duration, addressing employability and technical skills training and patterned after the Florida Department of Education curriculum model. Most programs are certified by outside agencies, for example, through the state university systems. The end product is an inmate who has acquired the technical skills and work habits necessary for successful reintegration into society. As the inmate reaches certain skill levels, he or she receives certificates with the final certificate from an approved OJT certification agency, which could be a university or the Department of Education. These certificates serve as critical parts of the inmate's job assistance packet upon release and his or her strongest marketing tools.

> *"The fundamental objective of prison labor is to transform unskilled . . . inmates . . . into productive workers."*

Formal OJT, as an integral aspect of the manufacturing process, develops industrial skills that can readily be transferred to the free-world workplace, allowing for a smoother transition back into society. Even two basic prison industry rules—showing up on time and working hard—instill the minimum behavioral conditions required when inmates integrate back into the work force. These "world of work" experiences emphasize self-discipline and responsibility while teaching time, resource and people management skills.

At the same time, it is recognized that there is some validity to the one prison industry criticism of training inmates using antiquated equipment and processes. Nonetheless, the opportunity to work on an industrial floor to produce goods and services provides inmates with the prerequisites to transition to more modern equipment.

> *"Adhering to strict educational and vocational training standards, inmates . . . [learn] all aspects of the industrial job."*

Adhering to strict educational and vocational training standards, inmates are measured against strict criteria, resulting in learning all aspects of the industrial job. This is accomplished by cross-training and progressive development from simple tasks to more complex ones. PRIDE operates its industries much like a free-world company—adhering to former Supreme Court Justice Warren Burger's "factory behind fences" philosophy—with the emphasis on quality, customer service and profitability.

Prerelease Workshops

A prerelease workshop, the second component in the process, is conducted for inmates within 90 days of their end-of-sentence (EOS) date and is geared to job readiness. To standardize the workshop materials within the various industries, each industry is provided a three-ring binder with presentation slides in two formats: color overheads and CD-ROM. The workshop objective is to help inmates make their plans for re-entry into the community. By the time of the prerelease workshop, inmates have developed job skills and a work ethic. Aspects of the three-hour workshop include completing an employment referral form, developing a reintegration plan with established, realistic goals, considering housing and transportation options and how best to use prison industry experience in the free world.

Some PRIDE industries, such as optical and dental, have high placement rates in which inmate workers often are recruited and hired into free-world companies prior to leaving prison. However, PRIDE also has sugar cane workers and male sewing machine operators, many of whom will not be able to find, nor are they interested in finding, employment in their current fields of experience. However, these inmates have developed skills that will be beneficial to them in other jobs. For example, an ex-offender worked in the sugar cane industry, which helped with his transition by using the training he had received in equipment operation.

After release, he obtained work with a land development company operating heavy equipment.

During the workshop, resources available within the state to inmates are covered. Available community or residential support clearly varies from city to city. Special needs are addressed to include human services, mental health treatment, and support and religious groups. Veterans are directed to local veteran affairs offices. PRIDE offers education assistance funds upon release if the ex-offender has worked for PRIDE for at least 90 days. Social and life skills include how to respond to criticism, handle hostility and resolve conflicts, as well as general work habits. The objective is to identify all possible services that can be used at no cost and can be beneficial to the ex-offender.

> *"By operating a sound [job] placement component, the likelihood of improving the reintegration of inmates into society is greatly enhanced."*

Last, the topic of budget is discussed with recommendations on how to create one and maintain it.

Job search development is discussed with emphasis on use of the state job service, temporary employment agencies, yellow pages and classified newspaper ads. This also is the opportunity to present interviewing tips, which in many cases, is a first for inmates. The session ends with a discussion of health and family issues, priorities, fears, special concerns and the need to get on with life. A dose of reality is offered to develop realistic expectations as well as the willingness to start any job. The form then is sent to Labor Line, alerting placement on the expected EOS date.

The Employment Referral Form is completed at the prerelease workshop. The form requires the address and phone number of where the inmate will live, if known, and present and past work experience, very similar to a job application. Accuracy is important, as this form serves as the conduit to the job placement coordinator. Under the plans and goals section, a discussion of obligations includes the requirement to check in with parole and probation, sheriff's office, etc. Housing and transportation issues must be identified. Will the inmate return to his or her former family unit that may provide shelter and transportation and other support? This option offers the most stable environment and the highest success rate by offering, among other things, moral and emotional support. Or is temporary housing required and are options available? With some cities and towns lacking viable bus systems, a precise mode of transportation must be considered. Labor Line will provide monthly bus passes if a bus option is the most feasible means of transportation.

Post-Release

A recent success story that reflects the ideal scenario in which industry skills are used in the free world is about James, who worked at a PRIDE furniture industry for more than 11 years and earned 45 skill certificates. Upon his release, James was placed with a company as a computer numerical control operator. The employer is pleased with James' training, ability and work ethic. During the first two months James worked with the employer, he received one pay increase, reunited with his family and obtained a driver's license. James is very comfortable in his job that helped his transition back into the community because it is so similar to what he was doing in the industry, contrasting with the changes that had taken place in society.

Clearly, one of the most important parts of the inmate's job effort upon release is to immediately call the toll-free number using the business card provided. The key phrase emphasized throughout the process is that cooperation equals job and success. Although the toll-free number is not staffed at all times, callers may reach a counselor on weekends. Inmates must stay in touch and go to their assigned interviews. Job tips addressed include the need to show up for the interview on time, have a neat, clean appearance; have a pen and copies of PRIDE certificates, and be ready to start work immediately.

The job search can be difficult for the average job seeker, but it is especially difficult for the ex-offender. The string of rejections and the frequently hostile and competitive job market will undermine even the best efforts of the job coordinator, who works closely with employers before initial interviews and divulges ex-offenders' PRIDE worker status to eliminate it as a barrier.

A key factor in the job search is Labor Line's list of firms willing and ready to hire ex-offenders. Additionally, coordinators are linked to the state labor department's computerized Job Information System and can review and match ex-offenders with available positions statewide. Placement chances are considerably higher if ex-offenders are referred to companies with histories of hiring ex-offenders. Working with several ex-offenders at all times, job coordinators offer varying levels of support based on individual needs, as some ex-offenders will need more direction and control than others. The product of this joint effort between job coordinators and ex-offenders is a contract that specifies conditions that must be adhered to during the post-release phase. The coordinator's concern is to find a position for the ex-offender that offers a decent starting wage and full-time work. Consequently, day labor positions are avoided. The average starting wage for these full-time positions in calendar year 2001 was $8.76 per hour.

> *"Without an opportunity to work in prison industries . . . , many inmates will complete their sentences in worse shape than when they began."*

On some occasions, ex-offenders are placed into positions not directly related to their industry training. Two brothers were trained in different PRIDE industries. Frank worked in the PRIDE mattress industry and earned 31 skill certificates. Because Frank had no family support and was homeless, the transition program provided for temporary shelter, a clothing voucher, public transportation passes, and most important, job placement. Frank's employer called the office on several occasions to say how happy he was with Frank's performance, to ask for additional ex-PRIDE worker referrals and to say he would refer other employers to the program. Frank's brother, Joe, was in one of PRIDE's textile industries. Upon his release, he joined Frank at the housing unit and also was provided with transition program support services, including a position with an employer using the skills he had learned at the PRIDE industry. Both brothers called the placement coordinator on many occasions to express their gratitude for the PRIDE training, explaining that they had always been "gangsters" in the past and how wonderful it was to have lawful employment. Their employers are enthusiastic and have sought other referrals.

The Importance of Prerelease and Post-Release Support

If one views the OJT program as one component of a comprehensive program, it alone is inadequate for the majority of ex-offenders without an association to a prerelease and a post-release/placement component. To achieve this goal, PRIDE allocates nearly $1 million annually to operate its job placement company, Labor Line, as an adjunct to its successful prison industry operation. Although recidivism rates are not the best indicator of the effectiveness of prison programs, they do provide one easily understood and commonly used measurement to demonstrate the benefits accrued by prison industry workers compared with the general inmate population. By operating a sound placement component, the likelihood of improving the reintegration of inmates into society is greatly enhanced.

Once placed and with support from the transition coordinator, the ex-offender continues to receive assistance as warranted in support of his or her long-term goals. With a weakened economy, it is likely that a percentage of ex-offenders will lose their initial jobs. However, Labor Line continues transition support for as long as necessary, sometimes placing the ex-offender in three or four jobs within one year. This sustaining element of job placement provides support through the most difficult first year out and sometimes beyond. Close interaction with the ex-offender's parole officer results in establishing parameters for the ex-offender to follow. Even with high success rates, the PRIDE program has both expected and unexpected failures, as a good placement, a positive work environment and support from the job counselor will not necessarily prevent re-incarceration.

PRIDE prepares its inmate work force with job skills but also adds the prerelease and post-release component. The prerelease component attempts to prepare the inmate worker for the cultural shock of modern society. He or she should have a plan for the time of release. But more important, the inmate must have a toll-free business card. The Labor Line job counselor must have the employment referral form to better assist the ex-offender. In many cases, the placement occurs in a Florida city far removed from the job counselor's location. The cooperation between the ex-offender and the counselor determines to a great degree the successful integration. The majority of former PRIDE inmates make this decision. Of this group, the recidivism rate is 4 percent, validating the PRIDE–Labor Line placement system. The failures can be found in those ex-offenders who, for whatever reason, have chosen not to establish a link with Labor Line by making that important call.

John's story illustrates that immediate placement in a position is not the end of support, as the ex-offender's first year has its ups and downs; he obtained employment within several days of release. However, some old friends came by, and John ended up using a chemical substance and subsequently failed to report to his job. Working with John and his employer, the transition coordinator was able to keep him in his job and with support from his employer and the coordinator, and enrollment in a drug treatment program, he has been successful for 18 months. Without coaching and mentoring in place, it is likely that John would have given up, not gone back to work and violated his probation. Mentoring and coaching in the PRIDE Transition Program serve as key elements to job placement assistance.

Nora's story offers the best example of industry training and support, as she is skilled in a highly demanding field. Nora worked at PRIDE's Broward optical training laboratory and upon release, was referred to an optical lab in her community. When she went for the interview, the company put her to work immediately. She has received considerable coaching and mentoring along the way and is in a residential transition program with a shelter that gives her stability.

Prison Labor Works

Without an opportunity to work in prison industries (or vocational, educational and other similar programs), many inmates will complete their sentences in worse shape than when they began. Most inmates returning to their communities have not completed high school, have limited employment skills, have histories of substance abuse and health problems, and have attained only limited proficiency in any marketable skills. Offenders may have difficulties with problem-solving, work habits, understanding what behavior is demanded in the workplace and interpersonal relations. Prisons and jails do not generally prepare offenders to be ready for work.

However, prison industries provides them with the ability to overcome many of these barriers and clearly has proved to be effective during the past century. The 1996 Federal Bureau of Prisons report on its Post-Release Employment Project (PREP) study analyzed 7,000 federal offenders who received training and work experience and offenders who did not, concluding that inmates working in prison industries are 24 percent less likely to return to prison. By including a post-release transition component to the highly successful state prison industry programs, further reduction in recidivism rates through improving the chances of ex-offenders succeeding in their reintegration efforts can be expected.

Prison Labor Takes Jobs from American Workers

by Tom Adkins

About the author: *Tom Adkins is the publisher of the online political magazine CommonConservative.com.*

You live in a typical working-class village. It could use some paved roads, and maybe a new schoolhouse. But money is scarce because jobs are scarce. You are luckier than most. You work hard, making desks in the town factory. Your boss wants to sell those desks to that new government office on the other side of town. After all, in your country, the government is by far the largest consumer. And a nice government contract would mean jobs for your neighbors.

But all government contracts are controlled by a giant government organization that has iron-fisted rule over all government contracts—price, quality, style, delivery, even what product to make or buy. And if has an imprisoned workforce, paying it as little as 25 cents an hour. Yet it "sells" their products to the government at predetermined—and usually higher—prices than charged by your employer. Your company makes better furniture for far less money. But the concept of "bidding for a contract" is not permitted by your government. Deserving jobs never will arrive at your factory.

A refugee's tale from some frozen province in old Russia? North Korea? A story shared between Cuban defectors at a sidewalk cafe in Miami?

No. It's America in 2002.

Jobs Lost to Prisoners

The organization is Federal Prison Industries [FPI]—aka UNICOR, FPI's official trade name. Born in [President Franklin D. Roosevelt's] era of social meddling, FPI nobly was intended to rehabilitate inmates by teaching them trades. Not comfortable using prisoners to compete with free labor, FPI could sell only to the government. But the government could buy only from FPI, creating a totally closed market.

As the government bureaucracy bloated, FPI grew from banging out a few license plates into a $580 million monster, with 106 prison factories and 22,000 inmate "employees" churning out gloves, clothing, coffee mugs, circuit boards, office furniture, safety goggles, printing, boots, pillowcases and plumbing fixtures—more than 300 items in the UNICOR catalogue, effectively shutting out vast portions of the free market. In fact, FPI is the 39th-largest government supplier, just ahead of communications giant Motorola. Almost every U.S. bureaucracy is required to buy exclusively from FPI. And every dollar sent to FPI is a dollar less to an American worker.

> *"FPI [Federal Prison Industries] takes jobs away from working Americans and gives them to almost-free prison labor."*

To make a long story short, FPI takes jobs away from working Americans and gives them to almost-free prison labor, then forces its own government—via the American taxpayer—to buy their goods, often inferior and usually higher priced. Is your blood boiling? You'll steam when you hear multimillion-dollar horror stories of this perverted arrangement from companies like Herman Miller, Steelcase or HON Industries. Or Mike Rau, owner of much smaller Ponderosa Office Supply, who tirelessly tries to sell office furniture to his local Venture County, California, naval base. "It's really been difficult to go out there and continually hear, 'We can't talk to you because we have to deal with FPI first.' How can you compete?" Indeed.

Lost are about 10,000 furniture-industry jobs alone. It's even more infuriating to hear workers—with jobs disappearing before their eyes—tell their stories. Leroy Webbs, a welder with Steelcase Inc., has nothing against inmates trying to better themselves, but lamented, "We used to have a three-man group [on his line]; now it's a two-man group. All of us wonder if our friend would be working next to us today if it weren't for the prisoners." It's a double shot to the working man: a stiff jab when the crook robs him, then a roundhouse to the jaw as the convict takes his job from behind the prison wall.

Dan Hennefeld, uniform coordinator for apparel workers' union UNITE [Union of Needletrades, Industrial and Textile Employees], estimates that 100,000 jobs have been lost during the last decade. Companies such as Alabama's American Apparel [specializing in battle fatigues], New York's Glamour Glove and Maine's Hathaway Shirt are "hanging on by a thread." Hennefeld wryly notes, "Many of these garment workers are single mothers. They can't all go to beauticians' school and do each other's hair."

Even inmates who work diligently toward a fresh start often discover their new skills are thwarted by the very same rehabilitation system. Inmate Steve Moore committed himself to rehabilitation, becoming a model FPI grad. After his 1988 release, he started Moore Superior Services, specializing in solving UNICOR's unending installation problems. Over 10 years his business boomed until, suddenly, UNICOR began ignoring invoices, eventually taking over Moore's contracts. "UNICOR could have used me to show other inmates that working for them is worthwhile and that you can prosper from it," says Moore. "Instead, UNICOR took the business I developed and and destroyed it."

FPI's misdeeds are legendary. It commandeered computers destined for inner-city schools and resold them on a Website. It hired inmates for telemarketing, complete with credit-card access. ["Now, Mrs. Jones, what's that Visa number?"] Some of FPI's faulty products also have raised consumer ire. As Stefanie Starkey, U.S. Chamber of Commerce manager of privatization policy bluntly points out: "Screws fall out, things don't work, things fall apart."

But the insanity doesn't end with FPI. State prisons, under Prison Industry Enhancement, are permitted to sell almost anything to anyone in-state, provided they follow easy-to-skirt rules. And skirt them, they do. Prison Blues, located at one of Oregon's prison facilities, makes blue jeans, sold right on their Website. They even export to France, Germany and Japan, raising anger worldwide. Their catchy slogan? "Made on the inside to be worn on the outside."

Fatal Flaws

Unfortunately, every job created on the inside is taken away on the outside. And every business prison labor attacks inevitably suffers one of three fates: they close, suffer or commit the dirtiest deed of all—switch to prison labor. When workers voted 90 percent to unionize Florida's Point Blank Body Armor, the company threatened, fired and laid off a slew of workers, then simply switched much of the work to prison inmates. Even worse, the company's body armor seems to be failing. A Point Blank vest recently failed a very public, New York Police Department test, and *Defense Weekly* cited major sizing problems, suspected in the death of at least one U.S. soldier. What would happen if all companies could outsource their labor to prisons?

Like almost every government bureaucracy in history, the prison-industry system lost its vision, morphing into a self-perpetuating money-making scheme, a simultaneous assault on U.S. business and the American workingman. And it's all based upon the concept of giving jobs to prisoners at the expense of honest, hardworking Americans. Can it get worse? Sure!

"Every business prison labor attacks inevitably suffers one of three fates: they close, suffer or . . . switch to prison labor."

In the face of withering criticism, FPI advocates are scrambling to "reform." Former attorney general Ed Meese, chairman of the Prison Institute Enterprise, suggests a quasi-compromise: allowing free-market companies to "hire" prison labor by proving workers are otherwise unavailable. Stop shaking your head in amazement. Let's count the fatal flaws.

First, imagine the new bureaucratic mess. Layers of pencil-pushing boobs arbitrarily will demand endless studies, testimonies, affidavits, paperwork, etc.

Second, free-market labor cannot defend itself against under-priced prison labor.

Third, prisoners will take entry-level jobs that provide that first rung out of poverty from welfare moms, among others. In fact, a father could abandon his wife and kids, commit murder, then steal that mother's job from inside prison walls.

> *"No matter how you slice it or dice it, prisoner rehabilitation never, ever should come at the expense of an American job."*

Fourth, workers who haven't so much as jaywalked will lose their jobs to criminals who have broken every law imaginable.

Fifth, America would leap into a human-rights quagmire by obliterating our long-time principled stance on prison labor. Today, the difference between U.S. prison labor and Chinese prison labor is merely 25 cents an hour. Our human-rights crusade would be a laughingstock.

The other excuses quickly tumble. Supporters claim FPI pays for itself. But at what price? How many jobs are sacrificed? AFL-CIO's Greg Woodhead commented, "If you want to incarcerate people, pay for it. Either make a commitment to law and order, or don't." As a final refuge, prison labor proponents claim FPI's recidivism rate is 24 percent or lower. But prisoners who mop floors and wash dishes have a 33 percent or lower rate. Clearly, structure is the key.

Try Charity Instead of Free Market

Fortunately, politics makes strange bedfellows. In this case, law-and-order and free-market conservatives find themselves snuggling up with workingman liberals. And so, supported by the AFL-CIO, U.S. Chamber of Commerce, UNITE and the National Federation of Independent Business, Reps. Barney Frank [D-Mass.], Pete Hoekstra [R-Mich.] and others formed such a coalition, offering HR 1577, the Federal Prison Industries Competition in Contracting Act, designed to open government contracts to free-market bidding. That's a nice first step. But exactly who still should surrender his job to convicted prisoners? For even the dullest thinkers in Washington, isn't it hard to swallow Ken Lay [former chairman of the bankrupt Enron Corporation] taking a job from a working stiff by running a drill press in cell-block D?

Despite vast policy differences, support for prison rehabilitation is nearly universal. But as Hennefeld observed: "FPI is training prisoners for jobs that won't exist when they get out—because prisoners have them." Then how best to offer something that prepares prisoners to be productive citizens? Try charity. Charity takes on assignments the free market doesn't want. Think soup kitchens, park cleanups or projects such as Habitat for Humanity, which rebuilds homes in low-income neighborhoods the free market won't touch.

Imagine if prison programs spent 70 years perfecting charity instead of honing a 70-year attack on American business and labor. Plumbers, carpenters, electricians, roofers, painters, even designers and architects would graduate, ready for real jobs. That's better than putting a screw in a wood block 500 times a day.

The bottom line is this: No matter how you slice it or dice it, prisoner rehabilitation never, ever should come at the expense of an American job. Ever. The practice is indefensible, and there are better alternatives. It boils down to a simple question: What honest Americans should sacrifice their jobs to inmates who should be doing time, not overtime?

Prison Labor Does Not Reduce Incarceration Costs

by Joel Dyer

About the author: *Joel Dyer is the author of* The Perpetual Prisoner Machine: How America Profits from Crime, *from which the following has been excerpted.*

If . . . profit is the primary motivation behind the ten-fold increase in the prison population that has occurred in the last twenty-nine years, then it stands to reason that the potential for making money from this business of "justice" must be quite substantial—and it is. In fact, the business of turning crime and prisoners into profit has become one of the fastest-growing industries in the nation, an industry with hundreds of billions of dollars up for grabs each year. Corrections is now the fastest-growing category in most state budgets, and each year, more of this taxpayer money is finding its way into the bank accounts of companies in the private sector. . . .

Cashing In on Prison Labor

Prison labor is [an] area where both the public and private sector are cashing in on America's 2 million prisoners. Unicorp, the government entity that produces products with prison labor, now has annual sales of over $500 million a year. By 1998, there were over 2,500 prison and jail industries in operation in the United States, a figure that reflects a nearly 500-percent increase in such industries in the last decade. Prison industries include everything from sewing to accounting to telemarketing to the manufacture of false teeth, parts for Boeing aircraft, and the logos for Lexus automobiles. As these last examples illustrate, it's not just obscure companies that use prisoners to cut their labor costs. Large well-known corporations such as Microsoft, Spalding, IBM, Compaq, Texas Instruments, AT&T, Victoria's Secret, Eddie Bauer, Chevron, and TWA, just to name a few, are all using prisoners directly or through subcontractors as a portion of their workforce.

The 1,310 industries in operation in the U.S. prison system accounted for total sales of $1.63 billion in 1998. There is no cumulative figure available for the estimated 1,200 industries operating in our jails, but it would be safe to estimate that the combined sales for jail and prison industries is in excess of $2 billion annually and could be as high as $3 billion. With many states, as well as the federal government, . . . considering legislation similar to the [1994] Oregon law requiring all inmates to work, it is estimated that prison labor could be generating more than $8 billion in annual sales within the next few years.

Of the billions being made off this captive labor force, prisoners are generally paid between $.20 and $1.20 per hour—less at private prisons and a little more in some federal- and state-run facilities. Imagine how appealing inmate labor looks to corporations, considering that these industries are generating an average of $14.54 profit per inmate-hour worked. In a foreshadowing of things to come, at least one company has already closed its data-processing operation in Mexico's *maquiladora* district in favor of a labor force from San Quentin State Prison. Other companies have laid off their entire workforces, immediately replacing them with cheap prisoner labor.

> *"Both the public and private sector are cashing in on America's 2 million prisoners."*

In 1998, moviegoers who attended a screening of the documentary film *The Big One* saw filmmaker and activist Michael Moore trying to convince executives at Nike to stop using sweatshops in Indonesia to make their shoes in favor of laborers from Moore's hometown of Flint, Michigan. At the same time that Moore was pitching Flint workers to Nike, Oregon state representative Kevin Mannix was busy telling the shoe magnate that his state could offer the company "competitive prison labor." But Mannix wasn't talking about labor costs competitive with Flint. He was describing labor costs more competitive with Indonesia, where 74 cents a day is the norm. If I was unemployed in Flint, I wouldn't be counting on a paycheck from Nike anytime soon. . . .

Avoiding Taxpayer Reimbursement

Prisoner labor presents yet another serious problem for the [private prison] industry's claim of saving the taxpayer money. Most people want prisoners to work because they want prisoners to have to pay for as much of their own cost of incarceration as possible. To this end, most states have passed legislation that requires a large portion of all the money paid to prisoners who work to go either toward offsetting their cost of incarceration or to victim restitution, or both. But once again, private prisons are using the out-of-state loophole to pad their own pockets with the money generated by prisoner labor that should be going to reimburse taxpayers.

For example, Colorado has laws requiring that much of the money coming from inmate labor must go to offset the taxpayer's expense and to repay victims. But consider what happened when Colorado inmates were shipped to a private prison in Appleton, Minnesota, and were put to work in a variety of industries. At one point, Colorado citizens were paying $26,000 a day to the private prison to house 500 inmates; this number was eventually doubled. Many of the prisoners—I can't report an exact figure because the state and the private-prison claim that my FOIA [Freedom of Information Act] request doesn't entitle me to such information from a private corporation—were earning money by working for several private enterprises that had contracted for prison labor with the facilities owner. Had the working inmates been in the public system in Colorado, taxpayers would have been saving potentially millions of dollars on the cost of incarceration as a result of this labor. But because the prisoners had been moved across state lines, the labor earnings, aside from the few cents an hour paid to the inmates, were kept by the private prison's owner.

This can be a very significant loophole when you do the math. Private prisons are often paid $5 to $7 an hour per prisoner by companies who use inmate labor. Of this hourly fee, the prison corporations often pay the inmates as little as $.23 to $1.15 an hour. As I said, I have been trying to get the exact figures on the Appleton labor for years, only to be refused, so here is a theoretical estimate of the kind of potential loss to taxpayers that we're talking about. Let's say that 500 prisoners are working six hours a day, five days a week for companies that are paying the prison corporation $5 an hour per inmate. The prison then pays the inmates an average of $.35 an hour. In this scenario, the private prison would be pocketing $3.62 million a year minus any expenses associated with overseeing the labor environment that would have gone to offset the taxpayers' bill for incarceration had the inmates been housed in a public prison in the state of Colorado.

Clear Abuse

And Colorado is not alone. As already noted, most states have legislation authorizing the use of money earned by prisoners to reimburse taxpayers. A source at the National Institute of Justice who didn't wish to be identified told me that as of 1999, only six states had passed laws to close this loophole. It should come as no surprise, considering the amount of potential dollars at stake, that when I attempted—through industry organizations and the Department of Justice—to verify the number of prison industries in private prisons that were not returning money to the taxpayers of the inmates' home states, I was stonewalled or told that no one is keeping track of such information.

Personally, I have no trouble believing that no one within the government—the same government that the prison industry tells us is "inefficient"—has been monitoring this clear abuse of the private-prison system. It just makes me wonder how many other loopholes that we don't know about are being used by the "efficient" prison corporations to exploit taxpayers and prisoners.

Prison Labor Exploits Prisoners

by Jane Slaughter

About the author: *Jane Slaughter is a Detroit-based labor writer.*

Start talking about "prison labor," and people tend to fall into two categories. One is appalled at the exploitation implied: workers locked up, overseen by guards, with no say in their wages, conditions, or anything else. But the other group sees a chance to "make prisons pay" and to get tough on crime. Back in the 1970s, Chief Justice Warren Burger called for turning prisons into "factories with fences." Today, Burger's words are coming true, with consequences that may be as serious for workers on the outside as for those who labor behind bars.

The number of prisoners who work for private, profit-making companies or state-controlled industries—around 80,000—is still relatively small compared to the skyrocketing prison population.

But the numbers are growing fast, urged along by advocates in government and by companies who see prison labor as a closer-to-home alternative to production in Asia and Mexico.

"It's about time we stopped being ashamed of our resources and began putting them to work," says Representative Stephen Matthew, chair of a Congressional committee studying prison labor. Matthew says his goal is to have half of all prisoners holding down inside jobs by the year 2000.

Changing Times

Consider these trends:

- a phenomenal increase in the number of people behind bars—1.9 million today, driving towards one percent of the total population—propelled by the lock 'em up mentality prevalent in legislatures;
- fewer and fewer good jobs available, as the supposedly "booming" economy creates mostly low-wage or temporary or part-time jobs (or all three);
- welfare recipients forced into low-paid jobs in competition with other working-class people, under the heading of "welfare reform."

Then recall the rhetoric that conservatives use to describe members of what they call "the underclass"—"welfare queens" sucking up the tax dollars of hard-working citizens, criminals watching TV in jail, likewise on the tax dollars of those same law-abiding citizens. Given all this, it's not hard to believe that policy makers have in mind a two-pronged "solution" to the perceived problem of the underclass: low-paid, poverty-sustaining jobs for the women, even lower-paid jobs in jail for the men. As one advocate mused in an Internet posting, "[Prison] labor is the carpet under which can be swept those who fall out the bottom of the system, and it's a profit center as well! . . . It seems to be the only government-sponsored program that 'deals with' inner-city unemployment."

Slavery Lives

In a collection of essays by prisoners, *The Celling of America*, prisoner Paul Wright, co-editor of *Prison Legal News*, notes that Americans mistakenly believe that slavery was ended by the Thirteenth Amendment. In truth, Wright points out, "slavery and involuntary servitude" were abolished, in the words of the Constitution, "except as punishment for crimes whereof the party shall have been duly convicted." After the Civil War, it was common for newly freed slaves to be "duly convicted," sent to jail, and then leased out to private employers. In the 1930s, spurred by Depression unemployment, Congress forbade the interstate transport of prison-made goods made for less than minimum wage, effectively shutting down the private use of prison labor. It was today's prison-building binge that once again sent lawmakers looking for ways to make money from convicts' work. In 1979, Congress created a program to help bring private companies into prisons. From 1980 to 1994, sales by prison industries, private and state-run, rose from $392 million to $1.31 billion, as the number of federal and state prisoners working in prison industries jumped by 358 percent. Some industry officials estimate that by 2000 prison industries' sales will hit $8.9 billion.

Some prisoner activists, such as Paul Wright, call prison work "slave labor," arguing that it is not truly voluntary. According to the American Federation of Labor and Congress of Industrial Organizations (AFL-CIO), 21 states have passed laws requiring prisoners to work, and federal prisoners are required to work as well. Just as important, taking a job can reduce your sentence, often on a day worked

> *"It's not hard to believe that policy makers have in mind a . . . 'solution' to the perceived problem of the underclass: . . . [low-paid] jobs in jail for the men."*

per day served basis, and not taking one can subject you to penalties that lengthen your sentence.

Even at the pitifully low wages paid, prisoners take jobs for the money. Alice Lynd, co-founder of a prisoners' advocacy group called Prison Forum in

Youngstown, Ohio, explains, "I have a friend who gets $17 a month for tutoring. People working for Ohio Penal Industries get as much as $45 a month. It creates a class system within the prison as to who's got money for the commissary and who hasn't." One prisoner doing data entry at San Quentin said, "The food here sucks and a can of tuna fish costs 95 cents in the commissary, so I am really glad to have this job."

> *"Whatever the nominal wage . . . prisoners see only a small portion of it."*

Courts have ruled that the Fair Labor Standards Act, which mandates the minimum wage for free labor, does not apply to government-employed prisoners. Federal UNICOR [an independent federal prison industries corporation] inmates are paid between 23 cents and $1.15 per hour, and up to 50 percent of that may be deducted. Private companies in prison are required to pay the minimum wage. Whatever the nominal wage, however, prisoners see only a small portion of it. Prison officials make deductions for room and board, taxes, family support, victim restitution, and savings for release. A Unibase employee at Lebanon Correctional Institution in Ohio, for example, makes 47 cents an hour for data entry, and a sewing machine operator at Soledad in California makes 45 cents.

Incentives for Private Companies

If prisoners have incentives to take prison jobs, private companies have equally strong motivation to locate behind bars. A publication from the Department of Justice spells it out: "Inmates represent a readily available and dependable source of entry-level labor that is a cost-effective alternative to work forces found in Mexico, the Caribbean Basin, Southeast Asia, and the Pacific Rim countries."

Company executives delight that prisoner-workers never get stuck in traffic (though they are subject to periodic prison-wide lockdowns). Nor do they receive benefits or vacations. And they fit well with companies' focus on "flexibility"—available when needed for surges in demand, returned to their cells, with no unemployment pay, when the market sags. Prisoners can be fired for any or no reason, including back-talk, and they are not allowed to unionize, much less to strike.

On top of these incentives, the government often provides handsome subsidies to entrepreneurs, such as leasing them space at very low rates or subsidies to buy equipment. An ad from the Wisconsin Department of Corrections asks business owners, "Can't Find Workers? A Willing Workforce Waits."

Perhaps the most bizarre rationale for prison labor is that it keeps jobs in the U.S. "We can put a Made-in-the-U.S.A. label on our product," one executive told a Justice Department researcher. Companies argue that prison jobs would otherwise be done by workers in Sri Lanka or El Salvador. The president of multinational Unibase, with workers inside three Ohio prisons, says that keeping work in the state is part of his "sales pitch."

It's easy to imagine a scenario in which a worker loses his job, commits a crime out of desperation, and then ends up working for his former company in jail. But at least he's got the job, not the foreign competition!

Good for Prisoners?

Occasionally an advocate of prison labor will claim it's good for prisoners (as opposed to state or private coffers). The idea is that prison jobs teach work habits to those who've seldom held a steady job. One study, for example, showed that inmates employed by Badger State Industries in Wisconsin had a 15 percent lower recidivism rate than other inmates.

But others doubt that prison work will help prisoners once they return to society. For one thing, prison employers tend to cherry-pick the "best" prisoners, those with work histories and good records. Many managers set up the hiring scene as much as possible like private-sector ventures, with applications and interviews. So those hired are those most likely to make it on the outside in any case.

Second, most prison jobs are specifically designed not to require marketable skills. The Justice Department passes along the advice of a manager at a South Carolina firm: "Keep it simple—put the least complex sewing jobs you have inside the prison." Alice Lynd points out, "Sewing blue jeans isn't done outside prisons, it's done overseas. When they get out they won't be able to run down to a plant and get a job."

> *"Most prison jobs are specifically designed not to require marketable skills."*

Third, although punching a behind-bars time clock is said to teach a "work ethic," the stultifying nature of the low-skill job could also carry the lesson that work is something to be avoided at all costs.

Hurting American Workers

With the American workforce already battered by downsizing, privatization, contracting out, and the dislocation of jobs to overseas factories, workers' organizations are becoming alarmed by the rapid growth of prison work. "Prison labor," says the AFL-CIO, "is being used today to perform work in both the private and public sectors ordinarily done by free workers."

Under the 1979 Prison Industries Enhancement law, private companies who want to operate in jail must pay the "prevailing wage." They must consult with and win approval from union leaders in the area; their industry must be one with no local unemployment; and the local labor market should not be affected.

But as the examples below show, these rules are apparently ignored:

- In Arizona, a hog slaughtering plant closed down, costing union workers their jobs. The plant then reopened as a joint venture between the Department of Corrections and the state's Pork Producers Association.

- In Wisconsin, Fabry Glove & Mitten cut wages and slashed outside jobs by 40 percent after hiring inmates at the Green Bay Correctional Institution.
- In Utah, asbestos removal companies say that prison labor has virtually driven them out of business. "We find it ironic that they are putting an industry out of business that they are purportedly training people to work in," said a spokesperson.
- Companies in the government-supply business say that UNICOR's rapid expansion has cost 2,000 jobs in furniture-making since the late 1980s.
- A private prison run by Wackenhut in Lockhart, Texas, houses a company called LTI which assembles circuit boards for IBM and Texas Instruments. Wackenhut built LTI a brand-new facility (using prisoner labor) and charges the company a rent of $1 per year. To top it off, LTI gets a tax abatement from the city.

   But before this cozy arrangement, LTI operated a circuit board plant in nearby Austin, employing 150 workers. The company laid them all off and moved its equipment to Lockhart.
- DPAS, a literature assembly firm, closed its facility in Tecate, Mexico, in favor of San Quentin.

Prison Jobs Are Not the Solution

Youngstown, Ohio, where Alice Lynd lives and works, was devastated by the steel mill closings of the 1980s. She helped found the Prison Forum group after Youngstown officials hailed the construction of a new "Supermax" prison there as a job-creation coup. Prison Forum has drawn up a platform on prison labor that would protect both imprisoned workers and those outside the walls. Besides banning the displacement of outside jobs, it would give prison workers the right to unionize and strike, or, at the very least, to report their grievances to an outside labor organization to advocate on their behalf.

Lynd is a Quaker whose long-time activism has ranged from union support to draft counseling during the Vietnam war. Her work with prisoners, she believes, is "consistent with traditional Quaker concerns; it has roots that go way back." Prison Forum includes a retired schoolteacher, professors of criminal justice and English literature, two steelworkers and the religious education director of a Unitarian church.

As an attorney, Lynd is able to work directly with prisoners while also taking education into the community. "People tend to think of criminals as people who are like barbarians," she says, "people who are outside the society. But most of them are going to return to society, and they may have a more difficult time than they had before to reestablish themselves in a constructive mode, rather than go from bad to worse." She wants to "assist by giving people hope, help them figure out how their future can amount to anything, how they will make it on the outside."

Unfortunately, she doesn't see prison jobs, in their current form, as a big part of the solution. "Some major plants will hire ex-convicts," she says, "but there are an awful lot of occupations where they're not going to.

"We need to do much more at the prevention end. Increasingly repressive prisons and longer terms are not meeting society's needs. Jobs, education, assistance to get off drugs are being shortchanged to try to deal with it at the wrong end of the problem."

Chapter 4

How Should the Prison System Be Reformed?

Chapter Preface

Every year, close to six hundred thousand inmates are released from state and federal prisons around the country. According to the Bureau of Justice Statistics, two-thirds of former convicts commit new crimes and one-half are reincarcerated within three years of being released from prison. America's prison system has become a revolving door, at great expense to taxpayers. On average, it costs states $25,000 per year to house, clothe, and feed each inmate. In consequence, reducing offender recidivism has become the central focus of prison reform efforts.

Many reformers cite cutbacks in prison rehabilitative programming—job and life skills training and education classes—as a major cause of recidivism. Unskilled and uneducated ex-cons are likely to resort to criminal activity to survive in an unforgiving labor market, they claim. Richard Freeman, a Harvard University criminologist, contends that tough-on-crime America has abandoned its "unique opportunity to alter [prisoners'] behavior and rehabilitate them to re-enter society and the job market as productive citizens." According to Freeman, "The ideal criminal justice system would release exoffenders who would find work in the legitimate labor market and make a positive contribution to their families and communities rather than return to crime."

To accomplish this goal, reformers have proposed that officials pinpoint offenders' personal "weak spots" as they enter prison. For example, if an offender is a high school dropout and a drug addict, then he should use his time in prison to acquire a general equivalency diploma (GED) and enroll in a drug treatment program. Resources would also be shifted to provide more assistance to ex-cons during the critical first few months of their return to society. Maintains liberal commentator Ayelish McGarvey, "States should 'front-load' existing support services to the weeks immediately prior to and following release, when inmates need them the most."

Of course, prisoner reentry reforms are not likely to be effective unless inmates are willing to cooperate in their own rehabilitation. Critics of such reforms point out that convicts have already rejected schools and the world of work before they turned to a life of crime. And many inmates ignore the drug and education programming that is currently available to them. Asserts Heather Mac Donald, a reporter for the conservative *City Journal*, "Offenders themselves stand foursquare for the primacy of individual over government responsibility in going straight."

How prisons should be reformed to reduce inmate recidivism and cut operating costs are debated and discussed in the following chapter. Education, drug treatment, and job training while in prison may help those released—especially those motivated to change—transition successfully into the free world.

The Privatization of Prisons Should Continue

by Samuel Jan Brakel and Kimberly Ingersoll Gaylord

About the authors: *Samuel Jan Brakel and Kimberly Ingersoll Gaylord are lawyers and contributors to the book* Changing the Guard: Private Prisons and the Control of Crime, *from which the following viewpoint is excerpted.*

The U.S. correctional system, which, along with the police and the courts, constitutes the official machinery for dealing with crime, is beset by population and cost pressures that have intensified since the 1980s. Reformers have suggested various ways of relieving these pressures. Some of their proposals target matters better left to those who manage correctional facilities and services. Other reformers recommend changing sentence severity and certainty, devising alternatives to incarceration, and delimiting the classes of offenders within the scope of such policy reforms.

This [viewpoint] examines an approach to corrections that is applicable regardless of the specific policies in place. In short, we defend a modest proposal: "privatize" parts of the correctional machinery. Privatization, we believe, would make the corrections system more responsive to the system's various demands in less time and at lower cost—that is, more efficient. Privatization also would carry the potential for improving overall quality.

Since its introduction in the early 1980s, the idea of delegating correctional functions to private companies has become a commonplace, if not established fact of correctional life. Overall, privatization of and contracting out for corrections has worked well. Privatization of corrections can save substantial costs in the management of prison facilities, in the construction (or renovation) of prison facilities, and in the financing of prison facility construction projects. Private companies also can finance and carry out construction projects relatively quickly—a special bonus at a time when many states are struggling to build facilities as fast as the inmate population rises. And all this significantly has come at no reduction in quality. Private prison construction and management often is of higher quality than that provided by the public sector.

Despite the evidence for these claims, there remains strong opposition to the concept of privatizing corrections. Some of this opposition stems from a philo-sophic position that holds it to be "just plain wrong." Sometimes the opposi-tion is articulated in terms of legal concerns, other times in symbolic im-agery ("Do we want to put inmates at the mercy of the ACME Correctional Company?"). Some opposition re-flects pure self-interest. For example, public-employee unions are among the most vocal critics because they fear union members will lose their jobs.

> *"Private prison construction and management often is of higher quality than that provided by the public sector."*

Much of this opposition is ill founded. Although unions in some states (e.g., Illinois and New York) have effected the passage of statutes prohibiting contract-ing out with private corrections companies, there are no principled legal argu-ments to support this selective curtailment of the delegation of authority. Argu-ments base on governmental philosophy merely substitute preconceived opinion for analysis, and the symbolic objections misperceive both the central social and economic experience of our country and public attitudes toward government. . . .

The National Problem

The "generic" problems facing corrections systems nationwide are *overpopu-lation* and *rising costs*. Many of the nation's systems are in crisis, although a few states have escaped these deleterious trends.

The 1990s saw a continuation of the steep rise nationwide, which began in the 1970s, in the total number and percentage of adults on probation, in jail or prison, or on parole. In 1990, 4,348,000 adults were under some form of correc-tional supervision. By mid-2000, that number had risen to 6,467,200—a 48.7 percent increase.

The adult prison population (i.e., convicted offenders)—traditionally the target of the bulk of the correctional system's efforts and resources—increased, along with the more comprehensively defined correctional population (all those under correctional control, including probationers, parolees, and jail detainees). . . .

Large, systemic problems require large, systematic solutions. The solution we propose, which represents only one of several possible (not mutually exclusive) modes of attack, is privatization. We recommend not a precipitous, wholesale divestment of the state's responsibility for correctional facilities and services, but a more gradual, quasi-experimental approach. Each state should consider, as an initial step, privatized management of at least three facilities, according to size and security, that roughly represent the range of adult correctional experi-ences in that state. When possible, the states would distribute the initial privati-zation contracts in such a way as to permit performance comparisons between similar institutions. For example, a state with two high-population prisons might privatize one and compare its performance with the publicly managed prison. Similarly, if a state needs new prisons, it might contract out the construction of one prison to a private contractor, who also would be responsible for arranging its financing.

The objective is to implement privatization in a way that will allow the states to learn from the experience. The idea is to introduce competitive forces into the current correctional state-monopoly environment to test the effectiveness both of the states' traditional "public" efforts and of the private prison-service providers. The ultimate goal is to build a competitive partnership between the state and private enterprise rather than simply to hand over corrections to the forces of the market. . . .

Potential and Proven Benefits of Privatized Corrections

Few would argue that incarcerating and trying to rehabilitate offenders convicted by the state is not the business of government; there is no compelling philosophic argument for government to divest itself of this responsibility and its burdens. The issue is instead pragmatic: What is the optimum way to discharge this responsibility?

Private firms must keep costs low and quality high or else their profits will fall, their customers will leave, and if the problems are not fixed in time, they will go bankrupt. The theory that competition and the profit incentive enhance efficiency has been tested in countless and varied settings

"Each state should consider . . . privatized management of at least three [prison] facilities."

wherein public and private operations have been compared. It would be surprising if corrections were different, but empirical investigation is warranted still, and we must also ask whether noneconomic costs render privatization prohibitive irrespective of efficiency gains.

Costs must be considered regarding three aspects of corrections operations: (1) the construction (or renovation) of facilities; (2) the management of facilities and programs; and (3) the costs of financing construction projects.

By contracting out to private vendors, at least in the short term, states can guarantee themselves cost savings in all three areas, because, in the tradition of governments' contracting with private parties for correctional services, contracts can be approved only if they save the government money. In an era when companies are still trying to get a foothold in the market, they are willing to take initial losses. Therefore, governments are able to obtain contractually favorable costs terms, irrespective of the long-term viability of these terms to the vendor.

However, it would be shortsighted for governments to embark upon a privatization course if there were no prospects for long-range viability. If the terms are not lastingly viable, the vendor will withdraw prior to or upon contract expiration. The state may be able to get another vendor willing to play the loss-leader game, but the process is sustainable only for a limited period. Thus, long-term viability on costs is ultimately in both parties' interest.

After almost three decades of experience with privatized corrections, there is strong evidence that the cost savings are both substantial and sustainable. . . .

The Quality of Private-Prison Management

Even many opponents of private prisons concede that privatization may save the state some money, but they perceive the correctional enterprise as a zero-sum game—if costs are falling, then quality *must* be falling also. Yet this perception is contradicted by the facts.

One of the writers of this [viewpoint] (Brakel) conducted one of the earliest studies on the quality of private prisons. The [1988] study focused on the . . . Silverdale facility near Chattanooga, Tennessee. In an examination of sixteen major aspects of prison conditions and procedures, Brakel concluded that the takeover of the prison by the private vendor CCA [Corrections Corporation of America] had resulted in substantial gains in the following areas: (1) the physical plant, including its general upkeep and cleanliness; (2) safety and security, in particular improved prisoner classification; (3) staff professionalism and treatment of inmates; (4) medical services; (5) recreation programs and facilities; (6) religious and other counseling services; (7) disciplinary procedures; (8) inmate grievance and request procedures; and (9) legal access. In the remaining areas, CCA's performance was roughly equivalent to the country's performance, but in no area was a diminution in quality found.

Brakel pointed out that the improvements achieved by CCA came in a setting where a great deal of improvement was needed. The county's own management record contained many glaring deficiencies, a fact that figured heavily in the county commissioners' decision to go private in the first place. From one perspective, these prior deficiencies might appear to diminish the significance of CCA's accomplishments. On the other hand, they might be interpreted to augment those accomplishments. The company was dealt a difficult hand at Silverdale: a dilapidated facility with long-standing management problems, situated in a resource-poor environment, contracted out at a per diem fee rate that left the private provider only the slimmest possible profit margin. The fact that the company was able, against these odds, to achieve overall institutional respectability within two and one-half years of the takeover can be viewed

> *"There is strong evidence that the cost savings [of private prisons] are both substantial and sustainable."*

as strong evidence of the private sector's capacity to contribute to quality prison management.

C. Logan conducted a more recent study of private-prison management in

1990–91. Already mentioned in reference to the cost issue, this investigation involved a 200-bed, multi-security-level facility in New Mexico for the state's entire population of sentenced women felons. The now familiar CCA managed the prison beginning in 1989 and built the physical plant.

With more detail than the Silverdale analysis, Logan measured management quality in eight standard "dimensions"—security, safety, order, care, activity, justice, conditions, and management. Each of these dimensions in turn was broken down into more specific components, yielding a total of 333 quality "indicators." Logan compared the results of the CCA management experience for the first six months (June–November 1989) against the state-operated situation one year earlier (June–November 1988.) In addition, he threw in a third point of comparison by replicating the investigation in a federal women's prison at Alderson, West Virginia.

> *"Surveys of prisoners . . . find that prisoners prefer private prisons."*

The analysis presents rich reading and is recommended to anyone who is interested in the subject of prison privatization. For our purpose, however, the main conclusion offered in the study's summary will suffice: "While all three prisons are regarded as having been high in quality, the private prison outperformed its governmental counterparts on nearly every dimension."

Many other studies of the quality of private prisons have been performed. In Great Britain, the director general of Her Majesty's Prison Services concluded after one study that the private prisons "are the most progressive in the country at controlling bullying, health care, and suicide prevention." The director general then took steps to see that the public prisons emulated the techniques of the private prisons. Surveys of prisoners also find that prisoners prefer private prisons because they are cleaner, health care is better, staff use force less often, and, perhaps most important, violence among prisoners is better controlled.

Security Issues

Prison escapes are rare events in public or private prisons. Despite the occasional sensationalistic media account, there is no evidence that escapes are more common in private than in public prisons. Given the high costs of bad publicity to a private prison from an escape, one would expect that, if anything, the rate of escape from private prisons would be lower than the rate of escape from public prisons.

The charge has long been leveled that private corrections companies are willing and able to take on management responsibilities only in relatively low-security settings. The implications are (1) they lack "true" corrections experience and therefore will fall short if they undertake the management of a high-security ("real") prison; and (2) they are cream-skimming by taking on the "easy" populations in an effort to look good in comparison to public corrections agencies which must deal with both nonviolent and hardened offenders funneled to them by the courts.

These charges are false. In the very early years of privatization, some states (for example, Kentucky) limited private prisons to minimum-security prisoners. Today, however, the most common class of prisoner one finds in privatized facilities are medium-security prisoners, and the housing of maximum-security prisoners in private jails and prisons is not uncommon. . . .

The Morality Issue

In some circles there remains opposition to prison privatization on the ground that the incarceration of offenders convicted by the state is a uniquely governmental function whose delegation to nongovernment entities is "just not right." This view is often stated more pejoratively, particularly in relation to vendors who are in the business to make a profit. "Making a buck off the backs of prisoners" is the phrase used to describe the presumably unseemly character of this business.

Although this position has some intuitive appeal, if judging only from how frequently it is parroted by privatization opponents, it does not stand up well to more-reasoned analysis. The mistrust of the profit motive seems distinctly out of place in a society whose social and economic engines are driven largely by this motive—indeed, whose creative (and moral) strength is believed to be a very function of this motive, collectively and individually. In addition, the notion that the quest for profit is somehow "worse" than competing motivations, such as power or convenience (to name two that have considerable currency in the public and in other nonprofit settings), remains to be explained. Last, it might be asked what the critical difference is between rewards paid out in salaries as opposed to dividends ("profits"), not to mention that all those who work for profit-making companies—in prisons, everyone from the warden on down to the line guards—are virtually salaried employees.

> *"There exists no plausible theory why 'private' managers of prisons or their staff would treat inmates worse than their public counterparts."*

There is yet the matter of symbolism that causes resistance to prison privatization. [Ira] Robbins, the ABA [American Bar Association] reporter, has written derisively of prison guards with the logo "ACME Prisons" on their uniforms. [John] Donahue and [John] DiIulio have invoked the White House/President analogy to illustrate what they see as the moral or symbolic bankruptcy in the idea of privatizing corrections. Donahue posits the "who should paint the White House versus who should guard the President" dichotomy, finding it self-evident that the former is a job for private business, whereas the latter is a function to be performed by public servants. DiIulio paints a rent-a-President scene in which an actor "President" plus an entourage of musicians and dignitaries of the "Medals Corporation of America" play out on the White House lawn the role of giving out the National Medal of Honor to deserving citizens. According to DiIulio, it is clear that such a scenario would not satisfy us. The appeal is primarily to our moral intuition, though Donahue brings in the complexity of the guard-the-President task as among the more concrete reasons for having a public Secret Service rather than a private protective force.

Satisfied Prisoners

However, the message of these illustrations is not nearly so self-evident as their creators think. The question that might be posed in response to Robbins' ACME illustration is whether citizens necessarily find the private-sector identification less appropriate or less confidence inspiring than the public-sector identification, even for traditionally "public" services. Does the Federal Express or United Parcel Service logo suggest to the average consumer a performance quality that is in any way inferior to that of the U.S. Postal Services? To the DiIulio rent-a-President example the response should be: let the President or other public officials do the symbolic acts, while private providers do the real work. The answer to Donahue's complexity argument is a rhetorical question: Is the public sector or the private sector better at handling complex, responsibility-laden tasks? If one thinks of the air-transport industry, the utility of government oversight might generate some consensus, but surely there is no call in this country today for the government actually to "be" in the airline business. Rationally functioning partnership between government and private vendors is what the prison privatization idea is all about. Opponents of the idea might be less resistant if they thought in more limited terms, instead of in all-or-nothing, moral, and symbolic propositions.

Perhaps the final find most persuasive response to the moral and symbolic concerns about prison privatization is the evidence that the prisoners themselves do not share these concerns. The Silverdale study, one of whose main investigatory components was a survey of inmate views, showed that the prisoners' dominant concern was whether they were treated fairly and lawfully. Precisely where the ultimate authority of their keepers resided or what logo was on the staff's uniforms mattered little to them. They had no beef with privatization at Silverdale because they were treated no worse and, in several respects, were treated better than they were led to expect from their experience in the same facility under public management or from their experience in other public facilities. There exists no plausible theory why "private" managers of prisons or their staff would treat inmates worse than their public counterparts: the motivations are to the contrary (mistreatment fosters discontent, lawsuits, riots, and so on), and the empirical evidence provided by the inmates themselves clearly confirms this conclusion.

Private Prisons Are Poorly Run

by Jenni Gainsborough

About the author: *Jenni Gainsborough is the director of the Washington office of Penal Reform International.*

Corrections Corporation of America (CCA), the nation's largest operator of prisons for profit, is celebrating its 20th anniversary throughout this year "at both the company's corporate Nashville office and at all of the more than 60 prisons, jails and detention centers under CCA ownership and/or management."

No word on whether the prisoners will be celebrating with them. However, a new report from Grassroots Leadership sticks a pin in their birthday balloon with a very critical look at the company's management of both its financial affairs and its contract prisons.

Financial Problems

It is no secret that CCA has had its financial problems over the years. It came close to insolvency in the late 1990s after it accumulated heavy debt building expensive speculative prisons and restructuring itself as a real estate investment trust. After restructuring again, shaking up its upper management and spending $120 million to settle investor lawsuits, the company now claims to be in better financial shape. The report concedes that there has been some improvement but remains unconvinced about the company's long-term viability especially as many states are trying to reduce the size of their prison populations.

For those who are more concerned about the public policy implications of the CCA story than the ups and downs of its investors, the company's failures as a prison operator and its successes in influencing penal policy at the state and federal level are the most worrying areas of the report.

For-profit prison companies like CCA have always presented themselves as both cheaper and better than the traditional publicly owned prisons, staffed by state employees. However, from the mayhem and murders at the prison in

Youngstown, Ohio, which eventually led to the company paying $1.6 million to prisoners to settle a lawsuit, to a series of wrongful death civil suits, and numerous disturbances and escapes, the authors document in detail a staggering range of failures of prison management.

- failure to provide adequate medical care to prisoners;
- failure to control violence in its prisons;
- substandard conditions that have resulted in prisoner protests and uprisings;
- criminal activity on the part of some CCA employees, including the sale of illegal drugs to prisoners; and
- escapes, which in the case of at least two facilities include inadvertent releases of prisoners who were supposed to remain in custody.

Many of the company's problems are blamed on its labor policies. Because prisons are very labor intensive institutions, the only way a company like CCA can sell itself to government as a cheaper option than public prisons while still making a profit, is by using as few staff as possible, paying them as little as possible, and not spending much on training.

From the beginning, CCA has sought to depress its labor costs by keeping wages low and by denying its employees traditional (defined-benefit) pension plans. One predictable result of these policies had been understaffing and high rates of turnover at some of its facilities. For example, annual turnover rates at several CCA facilities in Tennessee have been more than 60 percent. Another, equally predictable, has been the opposition of public service unions to the spread of prison privatization. Criminal justice reformers, trying to reduce the use of incarceration in the U.S., don't normally find themselves allying with prison guard unions but in this fight they are all on the same side.

Influencing Public Policy

Despite this opposition, CCA has been quite successful in recent years in influencing the public debate and winning the support of legislators. Of course, it is not hard to win legislators when you back up your arguments with hard cash. The company spends hundreds of thousands of dollars during each state election cycle to try to gain access and build support for its projects. At the federal level, CCA has given more than $100,000 in soft money to the Republican Party since 1997 as well as political action committee contributions to individual members of key Congressional committees.

> *"[There has been] a staggering range of failures of [private] prison management."*

The presence of J. Michael Quinlan, the former head of the Federal Bureau of Prisons, among CCA's senior executives has surely helped the growth in its contracts with the Federal Bureau of Prisons, and the expectation of further expansion as more prisons for immigrants are planned. In its home state of Tennessee, CCA has enjoyed close relationships with many powerful public figures, including governors. And the for-profit prison companies have their own trade association lobbying for them on Capital Hill—the Association of Private Correctional and Treatment Organizations (APCTO).

While all of that might be dismissed as no more than the typical business-building efforts of any company looking to make a profit for its shareholders, there are other more troubling aspects to CCA's behavior.

One has been its use of research from dubious sources to push its claims of superiority and cost-savings for the private sector. Much of it is produced by researchers who are either funded by the industry or are ideologically predisposed in favor of privatization. For example, Charles Thomas, director of the supposedly neutral Private Prison Project of the University of Florida who was widely quoted as an expert on prison privatization throughout the 90s, served on the board of CCA and received several millions of dollars in consulting fees from them.

> *"The U.S. certainly does not need companies with a vested financial interest in further [prison] growth influencing our justice policies."*

More recently, a study published in the *Harvard Law Review* was touted as an independent academic study of privatization. None of its boosters, however, mentioned that the author, in addition to being a graduate student at Harvard, is associated with the Reason Public Policy Institute, a division of the Reason Foundation whose purpose is to promote the privatization of public services.

Perhaps most controversial is CCA's close ties to the American Legislative Exchange Council (ALEC). ALEC is a powerful force in the promotion of the conservative policy agenda among state legislators. One of its major functions is writing model bills that advance conservative principles and working with its members to have these bills introduced. CCA has been a corporate member and a major contributor to ALEC and a member of its Criminal Justice Task Force. CCA executives have co-chaired the Task Force over many years. As a result of the model bills developed by the Task Force, ALEC claims credit for the widespread adoption of Truth in Sentencing and Three Strikes/Habitual Offender legislation. Through its support of ALEC, CCA is helping to create greater demand for its services as a result of changes in state policies that keep more people behind bars for longer periods.

Although this aspect of its work is not given a major emphasis in the report, it surely represents the most troubling impact of for-profit prison companies. With more than two million people behind bars and the highest rate of incarceration in the world, the U.S. certainly does not need companies with a vested financial interest in further growth influencing our justice policies.

As Grassroots Leadership's report so fully documents, CCA has little to be proud of in its 20-year-history. Unfortunately, the problems that have dogged it are unlikely to stand in the way of its growth, particularly at the federal level where its pro-privatization, pro-incarceration policies are mirrored by the current [George W. Bush] administration. Even at the state level, where the report optimistically suggests that declining prison populations will hurt the company, there are signs that cash-strapped state governments are again turning to the private sector to solve short-term problems without any consideration to the long-term impacts.

And even though CCA itself has pulled back from the international area after a number of well publicized problems, the model of prison privatization it developed is still being sold to nations in transition that can ill-afford either the social or economic costs associated with profit-driven prison growth.

CCA may believe it has much to celebrate. The rest of us have good reason to hold our applause.

Nonviolent Drug Offenders Do Not Belong in Prison

by Stuart Taylor Jr.

About the author: *Stuart Taylor Jr. is a columnist with the* National Journal, *a nonpartisan magazine that advocates reform of the criminal justice system.*

The uproar over ex-President [Bill] Clinton's abuse of his pardon power in some cases has overshadowed his salutary use of it in others—in particular, his commutations of the savagely severe prison terms of more than 20 nonviolent, nondangerous bit players in drug deals. These clemencies were long overdue palliatives to the cruel and irrational sentencing laws that sailed through a drug-crazed Congress in the 1980s. But Clinton freed only a fortunate few of the tens of thousands of nonviolent prisoners—mostly black and Hispanic—currently serving mandatory minimum prison terms of five, 10, and 20 years for relatively minor drug crimes. Thousands more will disappear into the gulag every year.

Hard Time for Minor Drug Crimes

This grievous injustice—which prevents little, if any, crime—will continue unless President [George W.] Bush leads a bipartisan push for sentencing reforms that combine toughness with fairness. There could be no better way for the President to show that compassionate conservatism is more than a slogan and that he has the courage of his convictions about redemption and rehabilitation.

The thousands who could be salvaged are people no more dangerous than Derrick Curry of suburban Prince George's County, Maryland. He was a community college student with $150 in his bank account and dreams of playing pro basketball when he got into trouble for the first time in 1990, at the age of 20. Under the influence of a neighborhood friend turned narcotics dealer, Curry did a brief stint as a delivery boy for a drug ring. It ended when he delivered a pound of crack cocaine from the friend to federal undercover agents.

A few months of jail and an intensive counseling regime could have shocked this kid straight. Instead, he got the minimum sentence required by federal law:

20 years, without parole. Most murderers get less than 10 years, most rapists less than five. "Punish him, yes!" Curry's devastated father, Art, then a high-school principal, told the *Washington Post* in 1994. "Put him in a boot camp, work his butt off, give him some training. But don't take his life away!"

Curry got part of his life back on January 20, [2001,] when [then-president] Clinton set him free. A few weeks before, Clinton had told *Rolling Stone* that "there are tons of people in prison who are nonviolent offenders," that "the sentences in many cases are too long," and that "the disparities are unconscionable between crack and powdered cocaine."

> *"One-third of federal drug prisoners ... are nonviolent, low-level offenders who pose little or no danger to society."*

That was quite a switch for Clinton, who for eight years found it politically expedient to have his White House and Justice Department squelch a succession of proposals to bring some sanity to the system. One of the laws the Clinton Administration had defended mandates that crack defendants (most of whom are black) must serve five years if caught with 5 grams and 10 years if caught with 50 grams. That's far more prison time than is required for powder-cocaine defendants (many of whom are white) who are caught with identical quantities.

It was not until after November's [2000] election that Clinton expressed any unhappiness about his own Administration's use of such laws to send people such as Curry to rot in federal prison. Clinton's hypocrisy and cowardice on this issue have been of a piece with his 1992 detour from the New Hampshire primary to preside over the execution of severely brain-damaged Arkansas death row inmate Rickey Ray Rector. After 20 years of watching Republicans win by calling Democrats soft on crime and drugs, Clinton had decided to ruin as many lives as necessary to sound as tough as any Republican.

Disastrous Policy

This may have been smart politics, but it was disastrous policy. A 1993 Justice Department study suggested that some 21 percent of all federal prisoners, and one-third of federal drug prisoners, are nonviolent, low-level offenders who pose little or no danger to society. That would come to more than 30,000 of the 147,000 people in federal prisons today. As Clinton slithers into infamy, the time seems ripe for Bush to forge a bipartisan coalition to reform our drug sentencing laws. The objective would be neither to free dangerous criminals nor to let minor drug offenders escape punishment. It would be to give nonviolent offenders such as Derrick Curry a chance to become productive citizens and kids caught in future drug deals a chance to work their way out of the gulag. It would also save billions of the dollars that we now spend to incarcerate 2 million prisoners. As our imprisonment rate has soared to several times that of any other civilized nation, so has the cost.

The time is ripe because public opinion is turning against the lock-'em-up approach, to the drug war, which has dragged on for decades with little impact on the drug supply and no end in sight. One sign of this change of heart was California voters' adoption in November [2000] of Proposition 36, which calls for sending minor drug offenders to treatment instead of prison. Another sign is the proposal by New York Governor George E. Pataki—a Republican with a hard-line history but a keen sense of which way the wind is blowing—that the state relax its harsh Rockefeller drug laws. And the [2001] popular movie *Traffic* has made waves by combining a vivid portrayal of the horrors of drug abuse with a powerful indictment of the drug war, which it portrays as a war against American families.

At the same time, some leading conservatives and drug-warriors have joined the near consensus among moderate and liberal experts that long prison terms for minor drug offenders waste billions of dollars and thousands of lives with little or no impact on crime. Even General Barry McCaffrey, Clinton's gung-ho drug czar, has said he is "unalterably opposed" to mandatory-minimum drug sentences. And self-described "crime-control conservative" John J. DiIulio, previously an influential advocate of long prison terms, had a change of heart five years ago. He concluded that we should devote more resources to drug-treatment and crime-prevention programs and to the kind of prisoner-rehabilitation effort that had been out of fashion for decades. "There is a conservative, crime-control case to be made for repealing mandatory-

> *"Any sentencing reform proposal should replace prolonged imprisonment with . . . mandatory drug treatment and education."*

minimum drug laws now," DiIulio wrote in 1999, stressing that while we should still "incarcerate the really bad guys," we should give judges discretion to send nondangerous defendants to mandatory treatment and rehabilitation programs. DiIulio now sits in the White House as director of Bush's much-touted Office of Faith-Based and Community Initiatives. He has no official role in law enforcement, but he does have access to the President's ear.

Treatment over Incarceration

No President will ever be in a better position than Bush, a conservative Republican who once had a drinking problem, to lead a bipartisan movement to help people with drug problems by reforming the sentencing laws. . . . Attorney General John Ashcroft, long a champion of harsh mandatory-minimum sentencing laws, could be an obstacle. But Ashcroft's public statements since taking office have been consistent with a little-noticed Bush-Cheney position paper . . . stressing drug education and treatment and omitting the usual Republican demands for ever-harsher criminal penalties. Perhaps Ashcroft, who has forthrightly denounced racial profiling, will come to see that the drug war's sentencing regime has had an even more troublesome discriminatory impact.

Almost 80 percent of the people entering the nation's prisons are black or Hispanic, despite studies showing illegal drug use to be equally prevalent among whites.

One conservative who still advocates long prison sentences for even relatively minor drug offenders is William J. Bennett, who was the first President Bush's drug czar from 1989–90. "Crime is down—way down—and one of the reasons is locking up a lot of people," says Bennett, stressing that many nonviolent crimes deserve punishment and many people convicted only of nonviolent drug offenses are in fact violent criminals. Bennett also expresses concern (as has DiIulio) that the liberal brand of drug treatment often fails because probation and parole programs lack the resources and the will to coerce long-term participation by the many drug offenders who will otherwise drift back to old haunts and old habits.

There is some truth to this. But it does not negate the 1993 Justice Department numbers suggesting that tens of thousands of the small-time drug offenders in federal prison have never been personally implicated in acts of violence. Bennett's concerns can be met by letting drug offenders avoid prolonged imprisonment only if they are truly nonviolent small-timers and if they go into drug-testing and treatment programs that are adequately funded and made genuinely mandatory by the threat of imprisonment for those who slip.

To be both politically viable and effective, any sentencing reform proposal should replace prolonged imprisonment with just such an intensive regime of tough love, often including months of shock incarceration and years of mandatory drug treatment and education. As even Bennett concedes, with the right incentives and opportunities, many small-time drug offenders can stay clean and straight. Let's stop taking their lives away.

Drug Offenders Belong in Prison

by James R. McDonough

About the author: *James R. McDonough is the director of the Florida Office of Drug Control.*

An oft-repeated mantra of both the liberal left and the far right is that antidrug laws do greater harm to society than illicit drugs. To defend this claim, they cite high rates of incarceration in the United States compared with more drug-tolerant societies. In this bumper-sticker vernacular, the drug war in the United States has created an "incarceration nation."

Converts to the Cause of Drug Decriminalization

But is it true? Certainly rates of incarceration in the United States are up (and crime is down). Do harsh antidrug laws drive up the numbers? Are the laws causing more harm than the drugs themselves? These are questions worth exploring, especially if their presumptive outcome is to change policy by, say, decriminalizing drug use.

It is, after all, an end to the "drug war" that both the left and the right say they want. For example, William F. Buckley Jr. devoted the Feb. 26, 1996, issue of his conservative journal, *National Review*, to "the war on drugs," announcing that it was lost and bemoaning the overcrowding in state prisons, "notwithstanding that the national increase in prison space is threefold since we decided to wage hard war on drugs." James Gray, a California judge who speaks often on behalf of drug-decriminalization movements, devoted a major section of his book, *Why Our Drug Laws Have Failed and What We Can Do About It*, to what he calls the "prison-industrial complex." Ethan Nadelmann, executive director of the Drug Policy Alliance and perhaps the most unabashed of the "incarceration-nation" drumbeaters, says in his Web article, "Eroding Hope for a Kinder, Gentler Drug Policy," that he believes "criminal-justice measures to control drug use are mostly ineffective, counterproductive and unethical" and that administration "policies are really about punishing people for the sin of drug use." Nadelmann goes on to attack the drug-court system as well, which offers treatment in lieu of incarceration, as too coercive since it uses the threat of the criminal-justice system as an inducement to stay the course on treatment.

In essence, the advocates of decriminalization of illegal drug use assert that incarceration rates are increasing because of bad drug laws resulting from an inane drug war, most of whose victims otherwise are well-behaved citizens who happen to use illegal drugs. But that infraction alone, they say, has led directly to their arrest, prosecution and imprisonment, thereby attacking the public purse by fostering growth of the prison population.

Almost constant repetition of such assertions, unanswered by voices challenging their validity, has resulted in the decriminalizers gaining many converts. This in turn has begotten yet stronger assertions: the drug war is racist (because the prison population is overrepresentative of minorities); major illegal drugs are benign (ecstasy is "therapeutic," "medical" marijuana is a "wonder" drug, etc.); policies are polarized as "either-or" options ("treatment not criminalization") instead of a search for balance between demand reduction and other law-enforcement programs; harm reduction (read: needle distribution, heroin-shooting "clinics," "safe drug-use" brochures, etc.) becomes the only "responsible" public policy on drugs.

The Facts Behind Drugs and Imprisonment

But the central assertion, that drug laws are driving high prison populations, begins to break down upon closer scrutiny. Consider these numbers from the U.S. Bureau of Justice Statistics compilation, *Felony Sentences in State Courts, 2000*. Across the United States, state courts convicted about 924,700 adults of a felony in 2000. About one-third of these (34.6 percent) were drug offenders. Of the total number of convicted felons for all charges, about one-third (32 percent) went straight to probation. Some of these were rearrested for subsequent violations, as were other probationers from past years. In the end, 1,195,714 offenders entered state correctional facilities in 2000 for all categories of felonies. Of that number, 21 percent were drug offenders. Seventy-nine percent were imprisoned for other crimes.

Therefore, about one-fifth of those entering state prisons in 2000 were there for drug offenses. But drug offenses comprise a category consisting of several different charges, of which possession is but one. Also included are trafficking, delivery and manufacturing. Of those incarcerated for drug offenses only about one-fourth (27 percent) were convicted of possession. One-fourth of one-fifth is 5 percent. Of that small amount, 13 percent were incarcerated for marijuana possession, meaning that in the end less than 1 percent (0.73 percent to be exact) of all those incarcerated in state-level facilities were there for marijuana possession. The data are similar in state after state. At the high end, the rates stay under 2 percent. Alabama's rate, for example, was 1.72 percent. At the low end, it falls under one-tenth of 1 percent. Maryland's rate, for example, was

0.08 percent. The rate among federal prisoners is 0.27 percent.

If we consider cocaine possession, the rates of incarceration also remain a low 2.75 percent for state inmates, 0.34 percent for federal. The data, in short, present a far different picture from the one projected by drug critics such as Nadelmann, who decries the wanton imprisonment of people whose offense is only the "sin of drug use."

But what of those who are behind bars for possession? Are they not otherwise productive and contributing citizens whose only offense was smoking a joint? If Florida's data are reflective of the other states, and there is no reason why they should not be, the answer is no. In early 2003, Florida had a total of 88 inmates in state prison for possession of marijuana out of an overall population of 75,236 (0.12 percent). And of those 88, 40 (45 percent) had been in prison before. Of the remaining 48 who were in prison for the first time, 43 (90 percent) had prior probation sentences and the probation of all but four of them had been revoked at least once. Similar profiles appear for those in Florida prisons for cocaine possession (3.2 percent of the prison population in early 2003). They typically have extensive arrest histories for offenses ranging from burglary and prostitution to violent crimes such as armed robbery, sexual battery and aggravated assault. The overwhelming majority (70.2 percent) had been in prison before. Of those who had not been imprisoned previously, 90 percent had prior probation sentences and the supervision of 96 percent had been revoked at least once.

Substance Abuse Causes Crime

The notion that harsh drug laws are to blame for filling prisons to the bursting point, therefore, appears to be dubious. Simultaneously, the proposition that drug laws do more harm than illegal drugs themselves falls into disarray even if we restrict our examination to the realm of drugs and crime, overlooking the extensive damage drug use causes to public health, family cohesion, the workplace and the community.

Law-enforcement officers routinely report that the majority (i.e., between 60 and 80 percent) of crime stems from a relationship to substance abuse, a view that the bulk of crimes are committed by people who are high, seeking ways to obtain money to get high or both. These observations are supported by the data. The national Arrests and Drug Abuse Monitoring (ADAM) program reports on drugs present in arrestees at the time of their arrest in various urban areas around the country. In 2000, more than 70 percent of people arrested in Atlanta had drugs in their system; 80 percent in New York City; 75 percent in Chicago; and so on. For all cities measured, the median was 64.2 percent. The results are equally disturbing for cocaine use alone, according to Department of Justice statistics for 2000. In Atlanta, 49 percent of those arrested tested positive for cocaine; in New York City, 49 percent; in Chicago, 37 percent. Moreover, more than one-fifth of all arrestees reviewed in 35 cities around the nation had more than one drug in their bodies at the time of their arrest, according to the National Household Survey on Drug Abuse.

If the correlation between drug use and criminality is high for adults, the correlation between drug use and misbehavior among youth is equally high. For children ages 12 to 17, delinquency and marijuana use show a proportional relationship. The greater the frequency of marijuana use, the greater the incidents of cutting class, stealing, physically attacking others and destroying other peoples' property.

A youth who smoked marijuana six times in the last year was twice as likely physically to attack someone else than one who didn't smoke marijuana at all. A child who smoked marijuana six times a month in the last year was five times as likely to assault another than a child who did not smoke marijuana. Both delinquent and aggressive antisocial behavior were linked to marijuana use; the more marijuana, the worse the behavior.

Even more tragic is the suffering caused children by substance abuse within their families. A survey of state child-welfare agencies by the National Committee to Prevent Child Abuse found substance abuse to be one of the top two problems exhibited by 81 percent of families reported for child maltreatment. Additional research found that chemical dependence is present in one-half of the families involved in the child-welfare system. In a report entitled No Safe Haven: Children of Substance-Abusing Parents, the National Center on Addiction and Substance Abuse at Columbia University estimates that substance abuse causes or contributes to seven of 10 cases of child maltreatment and puts the federal, state and local bill for dealing with it at $10 billion.

Drug Abuse: A Greater Harm than Prohibition

Are the drug laws, therefore, the root of a burgeoning prison population? And are the drug laws themselves a greater evil than the drugs themselves? The answer to the first question is a clear no. When we restricted our review to incarcerated felons, we found only about one-fifth of them were in prison for crimes related to drug laws. And even the minuscule proportion that were behind bars for possession seemed to have serious criminal records that indicate criminal behavior well beyond the possession charge for which they may have plea-bargained, and it is noteworthy that 95 percent of all convicted felons in state courts in 2000 pleaded guilty, according to the Bureau of Justice Statistics.

The answer to the second question also is no. Looking only at crime and drugs, it is apparent that drugs drive crime. While it is true that no traffickers, dealers or manufacturers of drugs would be arrested if all drugs were legal, the same could be said of drunk drivers if drunken driving were legalized. Indeed, we could bring prison population down to zero if there were no laws at all. But we do have laws, and for good reason. When we look beyond the crime driven by drugs and factor in the lost human potential, the family tragedies, massive health costs, business losses and neighborhood blights instigated by drug use, it is clear that the greater harm is in the drugs themselves, not in the laws that curtail their use.

Prisons Should Focus More on Rehabilitation

by Philip Brasfield

About the author: *Philip Brasfield is a contributing editor of the* Other Side, *a Christian journal promoting peace and justice. He has been incarcerated in a prison near Gatesville, Texas, since 1977.*

It happens all the time. They go out of their way to cut in line for the chow hall with looks that dare anyone to challenge them. Squatter's rights established three-asses-wide on dayroom benches are considered an entitlement. You're trespassing if you want to sit there. It's just the way things are. This Texas prison is the department where justice is criminal after all.

Shame and Worthlessness

Voting in majority blocks along racial lines on television programs ensures that only a select group of sports, video, or variety shows are viewed. The programs are so similar in nature and content as to become one blur of loud noise and offensive images appealing to the lowest common cultural denominator. It's a degree of bizarre tastelessness I wouldn't have imagined possible ten years ago.

Repetitive programming provides comfort to many. If you know what to expect, then you convince yourself that you're in control of your life—even though nothing could be farther from the truth in prison.

Tabloid TV dramatizes drab lives of mean-memoried familiarity, lives remembered and stuffed with remorse and recriminations. Time regretted, time served. It isn't uncommon to hear a home boy say, "Hey, that reminds me of my ol' lady." I'm aghast at the number of foul-mouthed women that seem to haunt the pasts of my peers.

It almost overcomes me. The worst is witnessed at mealtimes. The table manners are truly appalling. Lacking rudimentary social skills, a majority of these men seems to have inherited some ingrained terror of famine; something genetically imprinted into those portions of the human mind most associated with the lower primate. They behave as if each meal might be their last.

Loud voices bellow the mindless, perpetual profanity of misogynists; the endless come-on games, the crotch-grabbing, ass-slapping, cavorting and gamboling mixed with the gape-jawed, mocking, fun-house laughter. It effectively destroys whatever appetite I might work up between one gastronomical disaster and another. I'd rather skip a meal than have my blood-pressure rise.

I sometimes find myself despising this miserable bunch I'm surrounded by, reveling in their sacred worthlessness. It shames me. At my very worst, I imagine how they must hate themselves, how a bad day must begin each morning when they look in the

> *"People behave the way they do for attention, recognition, and acceptance. . . . They don't know any better."*

mirror and see a familiar face reflecting a fathomless inferiority—a terminal disease that seeps to the surface of their bandaged souls.

These are human lives that eagerly applaud their pathetic mediocrity as hallmarks of accomplishment: lives tinted in many shades of black, brown, white, yellow, and red, all vying for their moment of supremacy over the other. Everybody wants to be top dog. Everybody wants to call the shots and have more money, more power, more anything—as long as it's more than the one whose neck you're standing on. These are American lives. These are also lives in prison.

If I could take my meals alone, I would. If I could trade this life in prison for a cloistered life in monastery, I would gladly don cassock and surplice, vow silence, simplicity, and poverty for that single-minded kind of solitude that really entails just being left alone. But there's not a chance of swapping my bunk here for a cot at Saint Benedict's, so somehow I have to find more tolerance than I've felt lately. That's hard labor. It's easier to hate everybody, to imagine machine-gunning the chow hall in lieu of pudding for dessert again. Pass the sackcloth, hold the ashes, please.

Survival Tactics

People behave the way they do for attention, recognition, and acceptance from others most like themselves. They don't know any better. The fear of being alone, of living in anonymity or experiencing rejection—these are as powerful as they are dangerous. To be perceived as different, strange, or alien increases your chances of being seen as "the other" or as an enemy. You become a target, someone expendable.

As heard on Golgotha: "Forgive them. They know not what they do." It doesn't come easily. Who has achieved the redemption of greater maturity on their own? Or who among us wasn't dragged kicking and screaming into the relentless light of self-awareness—and once there, embraced the enlightenment as a kind of salvation from our former selves?

I think of my own becoming, the painful process of meeting the constantly morphing needs of my developing ego. My slow transformation marked my hide with an intaglio of scars that I carry into the beginning of my second fifty years. I'm told they give me character, but I believe it's the scars no one can see that most truly define the human we are always becoming.

If the kind of mindless behavior that so enrages me each day is exhibited for attention to meet the emotional needs of peer-group inclusion, then I understand. Though affianced to anger, the conditional tolerance I slowly achieve recognizes the self-negating, self-destructive idiocy around me as transitory. The mean edges, the crudeness and pettiness—these actions are repeated and relied upon until a new, improved, and more socially rewarding form of behavior is learned, gradually adopted, and put in place of the old.

This is the stuff of survival, the camouflage, costume, and face-paint each of us employs as our guise to make it through the long days and nights of our sad and lonely traverse of endurance in lockup. And what more does prison encompass, amid the stuff of human failure held in concrete and steel embrace, than the time to engage in one's never-finished business of becoming fully human?

Out of Sight, Out of Mind

Prisons are not a hot political topic these days. The United States is too busy being global cop, wielding its current form of international justice, to afford any internal scrutiny of its own homegrown version.

These days, nobody seems to care why we have over two million people behind bars, why they remain there longer and longer, or why we are no closer to declaring victory in the war on drugs or crime. Hardly a thought is given to what the keepers of the kept do to ensure the populace outside that it all works—that the experience behind those thousands of miles of concertina wire is of some benefit to somebody other than those who are given a club to wield, a uniform to wear, a title to boast, and a paycheck to blow.

Truth be told, when you're sentenced to prison, your human worth has long ceased to be of value to most people. Those whose livelihoods depend on your loss of freedom serve their own best interests by denying yours. They do everything possible to abort the chance of positive change and to eradicate the hope that in some distant future you'll leave prison and the power it holds over you.

If you're lucky, you have a few years after you are first locked up before family and friends abandon you in order to save whatever's left of

> *"Politicians . . . console themselves with the lie that says [prisoner] rehabilitation is a false theory doomed to fail."*

themselves, whatever remains of their own broken lives. If you're blessed, you realize sooner rather than later that the only one you can count on is yourself.

The keepers of the kept and the politicians who pimp for them care only for the bottom line. They don't give a damn about what happens to a man or woman inside, much less what happens to them on the inside. They don't care if one's behavior is inappropriate or self-negating. They're nonchalant about the self-destructive, the violent, the psychotic (except when violently restraining and forcibly removing them from general population). Out of sight. Out of mind. Craziness is its own contagion.

> *"Instead of being thrown away as useless, . . . people in prison should be encouraged and required to participate in [rehabilitation programs]."*

Politicians and their lackeys who bankroll this nation's prisons console themselves with the lie that says rehabilitation is a false theory doomed to fail. They claim that people won't change—and that people don't change because they can't. They say that most people in prison deserve to be there or subconsciously desire to be there. They tell us we need prisons for our own good, for our own protection.

So what really maddens me isn't necessarily the behavior I described earlier, I suppose, or the boys who would be men who exhibit it. It's not their wide-eyed ignorance and immaturity, nor their lack of sophistication that stirs up my anger and swells my intolerance like a sore thumb.

It's knowing better—knowing that people can change, that people do change, and given the opportunity, help, encouragement, tools, and information, people will change. We always have. Human beings are the most successfully adaptive creatures in the long and bitter history of the world. Change is how the human race has always survived, by little and by little, by tooth and by claw.

Prisoners' Capacity for Change

If you believe the politicians' propaganda, if you think change is impossible, then you need to throw out redemption. You need to fire all the preachers and make them find honest work. Close up all the churches and the schools. Set up re-education camps for social workers, psychologists, psychiatrists—and ban all the self-help groups. Give up hope. Give up on yourself and everyone else.

But people do change. I've seen it time after time. That's the problem, I suppose: When people change, so does everything else. They're no longer satisfied with the way things are, and that's a threat to politicians everywhere. People who have changed are able to recognize their shared humanity and its power. Those who become enlightened will accept nothing less than enlightenment for others. Change is doom for the status quo.

No wonder the promise of "change" is used so often by politicians and candidates to bait the unsatisfied and disaffected—then resisted and sabotaged every step of the way once their votes are cast. Change terrifies those with something to lose. But it holds no power over los marginales, those on the margins of life, on the edge of survival and time.

All things are made possible by change. Instead of being thrown away as useless, dangerous, and unfit, people in prison should be encouraged and required to participate in counseling, education, and job-training programs that are designed to facilitate change and to eradicate dysfunctional socialization. Once you get a handle on how human behavior works, then you begin to understand your own behavior, and you're given a tremendous sense of power. People in prison ought to be taught a viable, marketable job skill that will assure them the dignity of earning a living wage, which validates participation in our society more than anything else.

Prisons succeed by failure. They perpetuate themselves at the cost of billions of dollars each year and at an unimaginable human price. Yet there are persons of all ages in prison who want to change and don't know how. The present system, based upon punishment for the sake of revenge, offers them no hope. It's little wonder that so many people who leave prison today are worse than when they went in. They are unable to "make it" on parole, so they return. Yet how many of them could successfully be reintegrated into their communities if they had a place to live, a job waiting for them, a real chance of putting their lives together because they knew that folks truly gave a damn about them?

If the United States is serious about controlling drug abuse, confronting violence, and ending conditions that encourage crime, then those persons most vulnerable to and affected by these negative social conditions must be encouraged and allowed to change—to heal, if you will—instead of being punished for not doing so, often for not knowing how. Their basic human worth and humanity have to be recognized and valued, their potential nourished and invested in, not denied and denigrated at every opportunity.

For we are all los marginales. Without the prospect of change, each and every one of us stands in jeopardy of being pushed completely off the edge, into the kind of dark void from which no one will return.

Prisoner Education Programs Will Reduce Recidivism

by Monica Frolander-Ulf and Michael D. Yates

About the authors: *Monica Frolander-Ulf teaches anthropology at the University of Pittsburgh at Johnstown, Pennsylvania. Michael D. Yates taught economics at the same school and is the author of* Why Unions Matter.

If prisons were places people who have committed serious crimes were sent to pay a debt to society, and to be rehabilitated to return to society as healthy members of it, then at least the following things would be true. First, people who had not committed serious crimes would not be in prison at all. Drug users and persons with mental illnesses would receive treatment and would live in their communities, either at home or in safe and hospitable facilities run as public entities. Those who had committed minor criminal offences, such as shoplifting, would be given non-prison sentences involving counseling and community service. As much as possible, communities would be involved in both setting the penalties and organizing and participating in the treatment. Ironically, this was typically the case in American Indian communities, now so ravaged by the U.S. criminal injustice system.

The Importance of Prisoner Education

Second, those who must be imprisoned would be placed in facilities that were comfortable, safe, and clean. They would be provided with healthful food and given ample time to engage in physical activities. Except in the most extreme cases, they would be eligible to return to society as a matter of course, and their sentences would be such that their return could reasonably be envisioned by them, giving them hope and encouraging them to remake themselves into persons fit to engage in normal social life.

Third, and of greatest importance, persons in prison would be provided with and expected to make use of training and education. For people who are not literate, there would be literacy courses. For everyone, there would be a wide range of classes and programs aimed at helping those imprisoned both to prepare themselves for meaningful work and to begin to get a clear understanding of the social and physical world.

Finally, prisons would establish an institutional structure to ease the transition from prison to society, making sure that former residents had adequate services available to them upon release as well as decent employment. . . .

The U.S. criminal injustice system does none of these things. Quite the contrary, it is structured in such a

> *"The more schooling an imprisoned person receives the less likely he or she is to get in trouble upon release."*

way as to maximize the number of activities characterized as criminal and the number of persons in prison, as well as to ensure that as many persons as possible remain in prison or return there after they are released. In this [viewpoint], we examine, partly through our own experiences, the third of the above standards for rehabilitative criminal justice, namely, the education of people in prison.

Since most incarcerated persons in the United States are poor, their poverty often compounded by racial and ethnic discrimination, it is not surprising that they have had woefully inadequate schooling. According to a 1997 report from The Center on Crime, Communities & Culture, illiteracy among the nearly 100,000 juvenile prisoners in the United States is very high: "Ninety percent of teachers providing reading instruction in juvenile correctional facilities reported that they had students who [could not] read materials composed of words from their own oral vocabularies." As high as 40 percent of juvenile offenders have learning disabilities. Few juveniles in prison complete their education when they are released. And, in adult prisons, the situation is similar:

Nineteen percent of adult inmates are completely illiterate, and 40 percent are functionally illiterate, which means, for example, that they would be unable to write a letter explaining a billing error. Comparatively, the national illiteracy rate for adult Americans stands at 4 percent, with 21 percent functionally illiterate.

The rate of learning disabilities in adult correctional facilities runs high, at 11 percent, compared to 3 percent in the general population. Low literacy levels and high rates of learning disabilities within this population have contributed to high dropout rates. Nationwide, over 70 percent of all people entering state correctional facilities have not completed high school, with 46 percent having had some high school education and 16 percent having had no high school education at all.

Reducing Illiteracy Reduces Recidivism

We know from the works and practice of Paulo Freire and his disciples, as well as from the practice of revolutionary governments in China, Cuba, and

Nicaragua, that illiterate people can become literate in a relatively short amount of time. By mobilizing teachers for nationwide campaigns and training them in Freire's techniques (which, among other things, uses words intimately tied to the experiences of the people being taught), Nicaragua's Sandinista government made enormous strides toward universal literacy in a couple of years. Freire, himself, helped Brazilian peasants to learn how to read and to write in less than a year. There is no reason, therefore, why people in prison could not be taught to do the same before their sentences ended. Literate prisoners could be trained to be teachers, so it might be the case that relatively few outside teachers would be needed, and these could be mainly utilized to train the inside teachers.

Recidivism rates are very high in the United States, ranging from 41 percent to 60 percent, depending on whether we are talking about the re-arrest rate (more than 60 percent) or the re-imprisonment rate (about 40 percent). This means that for many people, prisons are a revolving door—when people leave, they know that the chances are very high that the door they are walking out of will soon enough be the door they are walking back into. However, the one thing that is most likely to prevent a return to prison is education. Nearly all studies show that the more schooling an imprisoned person receives the less likely he or she is to get in trouble upon release. Literacy programs reduce recidivism, job-training programs reduce recidivism, and college programs reduce recidivism. For example, "Inmates with at least two years of college have a 10 percent re-arrest rate, compared to a national re-arrest rate of approximately 60 percent." There are some methodological problems with most of these studies, mainly connected to the difficulty of imposing adequate controls so that we can isolate the independent effect of schooling on recidivism. But enough studies have been done and enough testimony taken from the persons in prison themselves to tell us that education does indeed work. As one prison student eloquently put it,

> I believe college education within a penal environment is not only a valuable tool for the prisoner in gaining self-esteem and confidence, as well as future employment, but it is advantageous to society at large. A college educated prisoner has a greater capacity to function within a social context. Once integrated, the ex-convict, educated at taxpayers' expense, becomes a taxpayer instead of being a burden on society (police investigation, prosecution, incarceration, parole supervision, and in many cases, recidivism). He/she now can function as a productive member of the community. Education is one of the best investments a society can make within a penal setting. . . .

A Low Priority

Given the proven benefits of education, one would think that it would be a high priority for prison administration and for politicians. Unfortunately, nothing could be further from the truth. Education has a very low and decreasing status within prisons. Everyday in the news, we read about juveniles being tried as adults and imprisoned in adult facilities. Once there, however, they seldom receive the education that they might get in juvenile facilities. And in the juvenile prisons, themselves, education is woefully inadequate, though imprisoned youth might be able to prepare for a high school equivalency degree (GED). In adult prisons the situation is similar if not worse. Data on education in prisons are not readily available. We searched the Bureau of Justice Statistics's massive website and found nothing. Searching using the words

> *"The trend in providing education for those in prison is negative."*

or phrases "prison education," "education and prisons," "rehabilitation," "training," "training and prisons," and a host of other similar terms yielded no information. The Center on Crime, Communities & Culture was kind enough to provide us with tables for "Adult Correctional Budgets 1999–2000." These, unfortunately, do not have a separate category for educational expenditures. In some states, these are probably included in the category "Treatment Programs," and while this is a broad area covering more than education, it is noteworthy that the vast majority of states spend less (and often far less) than 10 percent of their budgets on treatments of all types. These percentages are very low, indeed, when we realize that the fraction of all people in prison who have treatment needs is certainly much higher.

In reports covering specific states or types of treatment, including education, the limited amount provided is always highlighted. "Of the approximately 130,000 substance abusers in California's prisons, only 3,000 are receiving treatment behind bars." At New York's Rikers Island, special high school programs were begun for eighteen to twenty-one year olds, after the Legal Aid society filed a class action suit. One of the schools, Horizon Academy, has had some success in getting students through their GEDs, but there are many problems. Only five of twenty-seven teacher are trained in special education, despite the special needs of most of the students, and there is only one guidance counselor. Classes are frequently interrupted by various prison procedures, and students are always being transferred to other prisons before they can complete their studies. In Indiana, only two of ten state prisons offer high school courses, and in those that do books are few and usually woefully outdated. Louisiana prisoner, Wilbert Rideau, says, "Rehabilitation can work. Everyone changes in time. . . . Most convicts want to be better than they are, but education is not a priority. This prison houses 4,600 men and offers academic training to 240, vocational training to a like number." He adds, "Perhaps it doesn't matter. About 90 percent of the men here may never leave this prison alive."

Cutting Student Loans

If hard data on education are scarce, we nonetheless know that the trend in providing education for those in prison is negative. Already in the early 1990s, a California commission on prisons was decrying teacher cutbacks in the face of already inadequate programs. And when there was a choice between having an illiterate prisoner work in a prison industry or attend school, the work assignment invariably won out. Back when our prisons were far less full, Congress, in 1967, enacted Title IV of the Higher Education Act which allowed incarcerated persons to apply for Pell Grants, direct government subsidies for college education. By 1982, over 380 college programs were in place in forty-five of the fifty states. The studies linking education to recidivism show that the higher the level of schooling attained, the lower the rate of recidivism. Yet in the put-them-all-in-prison-frenzy of the past twenty years, politicians have demagogically attacked federal aid to people in prison, despite the fact that no person outside of prison was ever denied a grant because someone inside received one and despite the insignificant amount of money actually granted to prisoners. The Pell Grant program and college in prison programs were effectively ended with the passage of the Crime Control and Law Enforcement Act of 1994. Once federal aid was eliminated, state aid was also cut, and not just for college education. As of 1997, "at least 25 states have cut back on vocational and technical training programs since the Pell Grants were cut. In 1990, there were 350 higher education programs for inmates. In 1997 there are 8." To the extent that prisons are offering any education at all, it is increasingly likely to be computer-based "distant learning" or housed in programs directly controlled by state departments of corrections.

> *"People in prison are human beings . . . eager to learn and capable of considerable insight."*

Teaching Prisoners: A Valuable Experience

Perhaps we can add some immediacy to the above discussion with a description of our personal experiences teaching in prison. In addition, we can try to make clear why all movement to depopulate our prisons and to make them humane are so important in the struggle to build a democratic socialist society. We have been teaching at the State Correctional Institution—Pittsburgh, a maximum-security prison in Pennsylvania. Monica has been teaching since 1991 and Michael for the past two years [since 1999]. . . .

Teachers can give witness to what they see and hear and thereby help the students and workers with whom they come in contact to get a truthful view of the criminal injustice system. Similarly, teachers can tell the world a basic fact: people in prison are human beings, in the right circumstances eager to learn and capable of considerable insight. Our experiences teaching in prison have brought this home. Almost every class has been challenging and thoroughly rewarding. Challenging, because of the intense engagement with which so many of the students approach the subject matter. Our discussions (one of the students describes them as a "runaway train") are usually highly stimulating intellectually; the reading material is subject to detailed and critical scrutiny by the students; interesting questions are raised; and we leave the class energized and convinced that this is what education is really about. Many of our own assumptions have been tested, and we have come to appreciate the vast amount of knowledge and talent that is lost to the rest of us when so many human beings are locked up for long periods of time. Teaching in the prison is light-years away from our "ordinary" jobs as professors at an undergraduate college, where the majority of the students appear to take their education for granted. There, questions are often met with a deadly silence (or even occasional yawns), and the students' limited life experience and thoroughly distorted and uncritical view of their society makes it difficult for them to become engaged in the learning process or subject matter. In contrast, the imprisoned students quickly take ownership of the curriculum and become involved in course development and other aspects of the program. Many act as mentors for other students; some have been co-teachers; and some help organize discussions to ensure that everyone gets his turn to speak.

As instructors we are also constantly rewarded by the students' appreciation of our presence. We are ordinary people from the outside who treat the students as full human beings with important contributions to make to the class. The classroom provides one of the few spaces inside the prison where free-flowing discussions can occur in a relatively safe environment unencumbered by the presence of people in authority. And here education is not taken for granted. The generous welcome we get (usually after a brief testing period) reminds us of just how precious it is to engage in a learning process that helps free our minds, not further imprison us mentally.

Educating the Public

Our classroom interactions can be used to good effect outside of the prison. We can use them to tell the public that the vast majority of people in prison are just like them, with the same dreams and aspirations, the same good and bad qualities. We can use this to make the point that any of us could end up in prison, especially if we are poor and most especially if we are Black, or Hispanic, or American Indian. We can use our extraordinarily positive classroom encounters to buttress the data showing the cost-effectiveness of education for people in prison. And, we can pose an obvious question: why wasn't decent education provided to these men and women before they entered prison? It is certainly cheaper and more socially desirable to educate people than to imprison them. What we clearly must struggle for is a society in which education,

"The struggle to make education available to people in prison can be coupled naturally with a fight to make education available to all."

at all levels, is provided to everyone as a matter of right. The struggle to make education available to people in prison can be coupled naturally with a fight to make education available to all. We can show that current trends are doing exactly the opposite. It is obvious that a good education is necessary if one is to "make it" in a stratified society like this one. It is equally obvious, given the data provided earlier, that not having access to a good education increases the probability that a person will end up in jail or prison. And yet, what we find are school systems that are crumbling in many parts of the country.

> *"The more classes the [prisoners] take, the more they can envision themselves as productive members of society."*

Students in many parts of the country sit in classrooms with leaking roofs; others are housed in trailers; many do not have access to laboratory facilities or even textbooks; and there is a shortage of qualified teachers. At the same time, there has been a massive increase in funding for prisons, with hundreds of new prisons constructed in the last twenty-five years. Remarkable, several states have been cutting education spending almost in sync with their increased spending on the criminal injustice system, and, in some states, more money is now spent on prisons than on schools. Pell Grants were eliminated for men and women in prisons, but grants of all types have been eliminated for all working persons. This is a crucial point to get across to the public at large. Too many people respond to the idea of offering college education in prison with the argument that, "Why should they have access to it, when I can't afford to put my child through college.". . .

Opening Minds

If teachers help to connect the students to a sympathetic outsider and to see themselves once again as full human beings, the courses themselves can open the students' eyes. We have witnessed many "Ahaa!" experiences that signify a whole new way of understanding the world and one's own place in it and the tremendous excitement and positive energy that follows. From a radical point of view, such experiences should be at the heart of any education and certainly within the prisons as well. We have noticed that the more classes the students take, the more they can envision themselves as productive members of society. In fact, a remarkable number of them have come to us with proposals for progressive social projects that they want to undertake when they are released. They have also asked us for other contacts who might help them make the prisons more livable and humane places. And our lecture notes, copied articles, and books are widely circulated, so that we reach many more people than those formally enrolled in the courses. Sometimes articles used in our classes have found their way to students' family members or friends back home.

Prison is a naturally radicalizing environment. Good teachers can help to encourage a coherent radicalism, one that grasps the nature of our society and suggests collective ways to change it. Teachers can also promote their students to organizations fighting for radical social change. We have had many students who would make excellent community or union organizers and leaders. They will just need a chance to become such persons, and their teachers can help, by giving them contacts and recommendations and by acting as missionaries spreading the truths that we have discussed in this article. About a half million imprisoned men and women will be released in the next decade. These people could make a real difference in every arena of social struggle, including, especially, the one aimed at ending the criminal injustice system itself.

The criminal injustice system is an insidious thing. It reflects a deep-seated and systemic antagonism between the rulers and the ruled. This antagonism guides the system and dictates what the rulers will do unless actively combated. Unless we contest it, the criminal injustice system will continue to incarcerate larger numbers of men and women, disproportionately minority, under the most horrendous conditions imaginable. The education of the imprisoned will be neglected, or to the extent that it is addressed, will be made to fit into the overall trajectory of maximum capital accumulation and maximum oppression. All manner of corrupt individuals and institutions, including colleges, will try to get a piece of the pie. We hope that those who read this article will be encouraged to agitate for prison reform and access to meaningful education for those in prison. We hope too that they will themselves try to get into the prisons as teachers or even to begin programs such as the one Monica has helped to initiate in Pittsburgh. We can assure you that this will be an extraordinary opportunity to transform both yourselves and the world around you.

Released Prisoners Should Be Helped to Transition into Society

by Jeremy Travis

About the author: *Jeremy Travis is a senior fellow with the Urban Institute, a nonpartisan social policy think tank based in Washington, D.C.*

When thinking about the future of parole, I have come to this conclusion: It's time to end parole as we know it.

Reimagining the Parole Model

I come to this conclusion reluctantly. Parole boards and parole officers are frequently maligned and vastly under appreciated. Both aspects of the classic parole model—(1) the decision by parole boards to release someone from prison, and (2) the work of parole officers in supervising those who have been released—have been critiqued as ineffective, castigated as capricious, and caricatured as naïve remnants of an earlier era when indeterminate sentencing reigned supreme and the goal of rehabilitation was the foundation of our sentencing philosophy.[1]

So, for those of us who value public service, it is natural to come to the defense of institutions and individuals such as these who are frequently under attack and are trying hard to do their best under adverse conditions.

Yet the problem is not with them, but with the task we have asked them to do. . . . I would like to return to the proverbial "square one"—to think critically about the two functions we have asked parole to serve, namely, determining the timing of the prisoner's release, and supervising the released prisoner for the remainder of his sentence. . . .

---

1. The practice of allowing parole boards to determine the length of a prisoner's sentence has been largely superseded by mandatory sentencing laws.

Jeremy Travis, "Thoughts on the Future of Parole," speech transcript of remarks delivered at the Vera Institute of Justice, May 22, 2002, Washington, DC: The Urban Institute. Copyright © 2002 by The Urban Institute. Reproduced by permission.

The Release Process

Release by parole boards is no longer the dominant method for deciding when a prison term ends. In 1976, 65 percent of the prisoners released from state prisons in America were released by decisions of parole boards. By 1999, that percentage had declined to 24 percent, and is likely to decline even further, reflecting changes in our sentencing statutes.

Some commentators would look at that trend and argue for the restoration of parole boards, for the return to an earlier era. For three reasons, I will not make that argument.

First, as a matter of principle, I have concluded that the executive branch of government should not decide the length of a prison term.[2] The research showing that release rates

> *"As a society, we have failed to meet [the] fundamental challenge [of prisoner reentry]."*

often decline closer to election time—and can vary dramatically between gubernatorial administrations—shows that parole board decisions are highly sensitive to the pressures of the political environment. Prison terms should not be determined by shifting political winds.

Second, the experience with parole boards has convinced me that their decisions are too susceptible to organizational manipulation and arbitrary exercise of discretion to provide a pillar for a coherent system of justice. Finally, as a matter of political judgment, I find it hard to imagine a scenario under which discretionary release through parole boards can be revived in this country. So, I do not argue for a revival of parole boards as a mechanism for making release decisions. . . .

By writing parole boards out of the release decision, our sentencing reforms over the past 25 years have eliminated a valuable role they played, namely overseeing the process of preparing prisoners for reentry. Clearly that task is principally the responsibility of the department of corrections, another executive branch agency. But parole boards, as separate entities authorized to review individual cases for release eligibility, have served an important oversight function. They have continually asked two questions, "Is this prisoner prepared to return home?" and "What is the plan for his supervision and support once he is released?" My assumption, subject to proof, is that this oversight activity has held corrections administrators accountable, to some degree, for preparing inmates for reentry and creating a plan for their return to the community.

This is the kernel of a good idea that I would like to salvage from the demise of parole.

These days, I view matters of sentencing philosophy through the lens of "reentry." I find it useful to focus on the fact that, with the exception of those

2. Parole boards are appointed by elected officials.

few who die in prison, all prisoners come back home. It does not matter whether they are sentenced under indeterminate or determinate sentencing schemes, released by parole boards or by operation of law, they all return to live again in free society.

From this perspective, however, it matters a lot whether individual prisoners are prepared for that journey home. It matters a lot whether the network of supervision and support is in place when they are released. My exploration of the reentry domain has convinced me that, as a society, we have failed to meet this fundamental challenge. I am not saying that in some prior golden age, we did this well. But, it is clear to me that we are not doing it well now.

If you agree with me that preparation and transition planning matter, then we should think about whether we want to entrust that preparation solely to corrections agencies. I think the answer is no. Their priorities will always tilt in the direction of construction and security. If we were to create a robust oversight mechanism, which government institution would get the assignment?

My heretical proposition is that we assign this oversight role to two entities— sentencing commissions and sentencing judges. In this new world, sentencing commissions would take on the task of developing standards for the reentry process, and holding departments of corrections accountable for meeting those standards. Sentencing judges would be expected to create and review reentry plans for each person sent to prison, just as they now approve supervision plans for those on probation. . . . This sentencing reform would also create reentry courts so that judges could oversee the period of transition after prison.

Introducing the Reentry Plan

How would this work? Let's make this real by imagining the following statement by a sentencing judge in a determinate sentencing state.

> John Jones, I have concluded that I must sentence you to prison. Because we are a determinate sentencing state, I must sentence you to a term of five years, given your crime and your criminal history. If you demonstrate good behavior in prison, that term may be reduced by five percent, or three months, for good time credit. Whether you are released in five years, or four and a three-quarter years, depends on you. Whenever you are released, you will face new challenges, the return journey to life outside of prison. While you are in prison, you should begin preparing for that journey. In reviewing your presentence report, I note that you need assistance in the following areas—you should receive drug treatment, earn your high school diploma, and participate in a job-training program. Therefore, I have directed that the department of corrections provide you appropriate opportunities to participate in those programs. Over the next few years, the department and you may modify your reentry plan, and I expect to be notified of those changes.
>
> But there is much more involved than just attending programs in prison. For you to have a successful return home, you will need to reconnect with your

family, get a job, transfer your medical care to a community clinic, stay off drugs, and stay out of trouble. You have recently been introduced to Ms. Smith, the reentry liaison who works for a new entity, called the Community Justice Corporation and is assigned to my courtroom. While you serve your sentence she will have contact with the prison and with you to see how you are doing in preparing for your return. Because our state believes that successful reentry is important, you will be brought back to this courtroom about three months before your release. I expect that my orders regarding your in-prison programs will have been carried out. I will also review your discharge plan to see whether those connections in the community have been made. If not, then I will direct the appropriate agencies to make them happen.

So, Mr. Jones, I, or some other judge, will see you again in about four and a half years. Between now and then, I will get progress reports on your prison experience. In the meantime, you, your family and friends, the department of correction, the reentry liaison and a network of community agencies will be preparing for your return home. We want you to succeed.

Make Reentry Plan Standard Practice

Impossible, you might say. But a version of this colloquy is now taking place every day in the reentry court in Richland County, Ohio. There, under a pilot program, the presentence report for prison-bound defendants is translated into a reentry plan, the Ohio Department of Rehabilitation and Corrections provides the program services indicated, a newly created court-based position of "reentry liaison" visits prisoners once a month while they are in prison, the prisoner is brought back to the sentencing judge at the time of release and appears once a month in a reentry court.

What would it take to make this standard practice in a state? The sentencing commission, working with the legislature, would have to amend the sentencing laws to authorize creation of a reentry plan, establish mandatory judicial review of the reentry plan, develop a checklist of things to be done prior to release, and reorient the administrative supports for judges, prisons and post release agencies to carry out this new set of relationships. The sentencing commission would also have to develop a set of standards and outcomes for prison programs and require the department of corrections to report on its progress in meeting those expectations.

What are the obstacles? It is clearly a new role for judges, a new degree of transparency for prisons, and a new dimension of accountability for the entire criminal justice system. Judges will argue they are too busy now; corrections managers will resist judicial oversight; the public will be concerned that prisoners may get services that other needy populations are not getting; state legislatures will not want to pay for it. But to these concerns, I say, simply, remember we are in the world of square one. I think we could achieve significant reductions in prison costs, new crimes and substance abuse, while increasing the productivity of returning prisoners. So, if we focus on our goals and keep these positive outcomes in view, I think these obstacles can be overcome.

In short, I propose that we end the role of parole boards in making release decisions, but borrow a page from the parole playbook and create a system of oversight of the preparation for reentry.

The Reintegration Process

Let's turn our attention to the second part of the parole function, the supervision of released prisoners.

We should start by recognizing that about three-quarters of the prisoners now being released from state and federal prison are released to parole supervision, which goes by different names in different states. So, even though the nation has turned away from parole as a method of release, we still release most prisoners to some form of supervision.

Yet that leaves one-quarter of all returning prisoners with no supervision. [In 2002,] U.S. prisons will release about 150,000 individuals unconditionally, just about the same number as we released in total during 1975. They have no legal status; they report to no parole officer; they observe no special conditions. For them, the question is not whether parole should be abolished; the question is why it doesn't exist.

Perhaps some of those individuals require neither supervision nor transitional services. Think of a prisoner who finishes a one-year mandatory minimum who has family, job, home and a supportive network waiting for him. Should he get no transitional support? Perhaps some of them are in dire need of both supervision and services. Think, for example, of a mentally ill prisoner whose term has expired. Should no one be responsible for helping his transition home? Perhaps some of them pose particular risks to society, and require close supervision by a government agent with law enforcement powers. Think, for example, of a violent individual who has been in solitary confinement, has been denied parole, but has maxed out and must be released. Should no one be responsible for supervising him after he gets out of prison?

These are very difficult questions. While I do not pretend to have answers to all of them, I am troubled by conversations I have had with a number of high ranking corrections managers over the years. They frankly acknowledge that, whatever we might think about the adequacy of their efforts to prepare prisoners for release, they feel the least obligation to prepare those who are released unconditionally.

> *"[By establishing reentry courts] we could achieve significant reductions in prison costs, new crimes and substance abuse."*

Some said they have no special obligation to secure employment, notify family, arrange for drug treatment, provide identification, or find housing for those prisoners who are simply released. They have no obligation to notify the police or anyone else. In this view, the prisons have done their job in keeping the prisoners safe and the state's responsibility ends when the prisoner leaves the prison grounds.

The Government's Obligation

Clearly this is unsatisfying. It seems to me that, as a matter of principle, the government has an obligation—to the prisoner, his family, his community and the general public—to facilitate a smooth and safe transition for every returning prisoner.

Let's put some flesh on this skeleton. What does it mean for the government to take on this responsibility?

I [began] . . . with the words, "It's time to end parole as we know it," consciously adapting the rallying cry of welfare reform.[3] I am fascinated by the parallels between welfare reform and what I see as the emerging contours of an era of justice reform. I think these parallels help us answer this question.

The welfare reform movement has been characterized by three innovative ideas. First is the concept of devolution, the idea that governmental decisions should be moved closer to the communities directly affected by those decisions. Second is the idea that reform can be accelerated through financial incentives, the notion that government should set performance goals and share the savings if those goals are met. Third is the focus on moving the client to a state of greater independence, through a mix of traditional and nontraditional interventions. All three of these ideas apply to the work of justice reformers, particularly as we envision a world beyond parole.

Let's look at the last of these first. I think the goal of everyone involved in the reentry process—the individual prisoner, his family, his community and the agencies of government—should be to improve the chances of successful reintegration for each returning prisoner. This means re-establishing (or, as the case may be, establishing) positive connections between the returning prisoner and his family, the world of work and the institutions of community.

Embracing this goal does not diminish the importance of a second goal, crime reduction. But we should recognize that reintegration is a separate objective. Improving reintegration outcomes may or may not be associated with crime reduction, but these are ultimately the more important goals. The literature on desistance shows that the crime producing years pass, and most ex-offenders live long lives after their criminal careers are over. So for millions of ex-felons amongst us who live crime free lives, the policy question is whether they are productive members of our society.

> *"The government has an obligation . . . to facilitate a smooth and safe transition for every returning prisoner."*

3. In 1996 time limits and other restrictions were placed on federal welfare assistance.

Chapter 4

Increasing the Odds of a Successful Transition

Focusing on these two goals—reintegration and crime reduction—requires us to focus intensely on the days, weeks and months immediately following the release from prison. This period poses the greatest risk of failure. Rearrest rates are high. Rates of relapse to substance abuse are high. Rates of homelessness are high. . . . The time right after release is disorienting, fraught with danger, and poorly managed.

When we look at this state of affairs from the safety of square one, this seems quite strange. In the period of time up to the prisoner's release, New Yorkers spend about $2,400 a month on each prisoner. He has adequate health care, a roof over his head, three meals a day, lots of supervision, access to a library, perhaps access to programs to deal with his needs. Without painting a rosy picture of prison life, we must acknowledge that certain basics are taken care of. Yet on the day of his release, we spend from zero dollars (for unconditional releases) to about $265 a month (about one-tenth the prison costs) in criminal justice dollars for an average parolee in New York. Most of this expenditure goes for supervision. Little of it goes for housing, medical attention, drug treatment or other programs, or work, although released prisoners often consume significant public dollars whey they show up at homeless shelters, get rearrested, or access benefits and social services.

> *"[Resources should] focus intensely on the days, weeks and months immediately following the release from prison."*

Let's imagine a world in which we spent the same amount of money per month during the first three months after release as we do for the three months prior to release. This would cost about $7,000 for every prisoner returning home. We now spend almost that amount for the entire period of parole supervision in New York, but let's front-load this expenditure to the first three months back in the community. This money would support transitional housing, if needed, employment if no other job could be found, drug treatment, medical attention, family counseling—in short, whatever was required to increase the odds of successful transition. Part of this money would also fund a community-based support network. This network would include case managers serving as advocates for the returning prisoner, and an organization of ex-offenders who had gone straight and could provide invaluable guidance to the latest returning prisoner.

What is the goal of these activities? To help the returning prisoner make the transition to the free world, get back on his feet, find the positive support systems that might work for him, stay out of crime, stay sober and increase the chances of successful reintegration. Not everyone will need this kind of support; some may need it more than others; some may reject it and quickly return to a life of anti-social behavior. . . .

Conditions of Release

I have said nothing about the remainder of the prison sentence, the conditions of supervision, or revocations of parole. I think it is appropriate to require that returning prisoners abide by some conditions of their release. These conditions should be few in number, readily enforceable, supported by strong research, and strictly tied to the two goals of reintegration and crime reduction.

But what should we do if these conditions are not met? Our current answer to this question is very unsatisfactory. In most states, we say that a parolee may be returned to prison for the remainder of his sentence if he violates a condition of his parole. We have created a second sentencing system, one where there is no relationship between punishment and offense. This sentencing system is even more arbitrary and opaque than the system of indeterminate sentencing that attracted the critique of liberals and conservatives thirty years ago. This sentencing system now sends over 200,000 people to state prison each year, over a third of all prison admissions. . . .

In short, I believe we should apply the principles of structured sentencing to this backend sentencing—to state clearly the behaviors that warrant revocation of parole, the reasons for upward and downward departures, and the sanctions that may be imposed for each violation. I also believe that backend sentencing is best administered by a judge sitting in a reentry court, not an agent of the executive branch.

Yet even these reforms would miss a more fundamental point. Why is there any state prison time left to be served? If someone violates these new conditions of release, and the violation warrants the deprivation of liberty, why not sentence the individual to the local jail? Why do we hold onto the antiquated belief that time is still "owed" to the state?

Recidivism Reduction and Cost Savings

In my view, there are only two reasons to deprive someone of liberty after he has been released from prison. First, if he has committed a new crime, in which case that crime should be prosecuted like any other crime, not under the guise of a parole violation. Second, if he has failed to abide by a critical component of a transition plan, such as attending drug treatment program, staying away from an intimate partner if there is a history of abuse, working at an approved job or staying drug free. I would cap these sanctions at a low level, perhaps five days in jail, and cap the exposure to these sanctions to the first three months after release from prison, renewable in three month extensions up to a year, upon a showing that continued judicial supervision is needed to reduce the public safety risk. By considerably shortening the period of transition between three and twelve months, we could

> *"We could take all the money now spent on parole . . . and create . . . a system of intensive transitional support."*

take all the money now spent on parole, front-load it, and create, in effect, a system of intensive transitional support, with focused supervision.

After this period of time, this mix of intensive support and supervision would be over and the individual would be free to get on with his life, subject only to any ongoing prohibitions imposed at the time of sentence (e.g., bars on employment or requirements to register as a sex offender).

> *"We have ended welfare as we knew it. We can also end parole as we know it."*

So the first lesson from welfare reform is that justice reform should focus on the transition to independence. Because the critical period is the time right after release from prison, resources should be focused there, and reintegration, as well as recidivism reduction, should be the goal.

The second lesson from welfare reform is that the government should establish financial incentives for successful innovation. The application of this lesson to our discussion is clear. I would argue that a front-loaded system of transitional support, with reduced exposure to new deprivations of liberty, overseen by a reentry court, would reduce the flow of parole violators being sent back to prison. If this happens, then these savings should be made available to the communities that are experimenting with this justice innovation. In the welfare reform experience, this kind of financial incentive resulted in important and effective new programs that moved hundreds of thousands of welfare recipients off the welfare rolls. I think the justice reform I have outlined could have similar results, moving more ex-prisoners to productive pathways of social reintegration. . . .

The System at Work

In closing, let's imagine how this new system of support and supervision might work. . . . [The hypothetical] John Jones . . . received a five-year prison sentence. Because he is a resident of the 79th Precinct, he begins working with his reentry liaison from the Bedford Stuyvesant Office of the Community Justice Corporation the day he is sent to prison. As his release date draws closer, that work intensifies. He is transferred to a prerelease facility closer to his community. The reentry liaison makes sure he has housing, a job, drug treatment, family and peer group support. If need be, these services are paid for by the Corporation. The reentry liaison knows Bedford Stuyvesant well. He works there; he only supervises individuals who live there. He knows the community organizations and individuals that can be helpful. He knows the risks like the back of his hand.

When John is released from prison, he is brought to the reentry court (ideally located in Bedford Stuyvesant), where the judge reiterates the expectations under the reentry plan. In the court are his reentry liaison, family, service providers and others who are committed to working with John. He returns to court once a month for three months and is in frequent contact with his reentry liaison. The court monitors his progress. If he is rearrested, all bets are off. If he fails to meet a condition of his transition plan, he is subject to a series of graduated sanctions that the judge must apply, up to five days in the local jail. If he poses a serious crime risk, his transition period may be extended, up to a year. If he completes his transition plan, there is a court ceremony commemorating his accomplishment. At this ceremony, he will be given an application to restore his right to vote.

I realize this is an ambitious vision of justice reform. But remember we are speaking from the safety of square one. More to the point, remember we are speaking against the backdrop of welfare reform. We have ended welfare as we knew it. We can also end parole as we know it. We simply need to find common ground and common purpose. For me, the common ground is the focus on the realities of prisoner reentry. And the common purpose is to reduce our nation's reliance on incarceration, while promoting successful reintegration of returning prisoners, and enhancing community safety. I think we can accomplish all three of those worthy goals.

Organizations to Contact

The editors have compiled the following list of organizations concerned with the issues debated in this book. The descriptions are derived from materials provided by the organizations. All have publications or information available for interested readers. The list was compiled on the date of publication of the present volume; names, addresses, phone and fax numbers, and e-mail and Internet addresses may change. Be aware that many organizations may take several weeks or longer to respond to inquiries, so allow as much time as possible.

American Civil Liberties Union (ACLU)
National Prison Project, 733 Fifteenth St. NW, Suite 620, Washington, DC 20005
(202) 393-4930 • fax: (202) 393-4931
e-mail: aclu@aclu.org • Web site: www.aclu.org

Formed in 1972, the ACLU's National Prison Project is a resource center that works to protect the Eighth Amendment rights of adult and juvenile offenders. It opposes electronic monitoring of offenders and the privatization of prisons. The project publishes the quarterly *National Prison Project Journal* and various booklets.

American Correctional Association (ACA)
4830 Forbes Blvd., Lanham, MD 20706-4322
(800) 222-5646 • (301) 918-1900
e-mail: jeffw@aca.org • Web site: www.aca.org

ACA is committed to improving national and international correctional policy and to promoting the professional development of those working in the field of corrections. It offers a variety of books and courses on the criminal justice system. ACA publishes the bimonthly magazine *Corrections Today.*

Amnesty International (AI)
322 Eighth Ave., New York, NY 10001
(212) 807-8400 • fax: (212) 627-1451
e-mail: aimember@aiusa.org • Web site: www.amnesty-usa.org

AI is an independent worldwide movement working for the release of all prisoners of conscience, fair and prompt trials for political prisoners, and an end to torture and executions. AI is funded by donations from its members and supporters throughout the world. It publishes books, reports, and the bimonthly *Amnesty International Newsletter.*

Cato Institute
1000 Massachusetts Ave. NW, Washington, DC 20001-5403
(202) 842-0200 • fax: (202) 842-3490
e-mail: cato@cato.org • Web site: www.cato.org

Cato is a libertarian research foundation working to limit the role of government and protect individual liberties. It contends that too many Americans are incarcerated in the failing war on drugs. The institute has evaluated government criminal justice policies and offered prison reform proposals in its publication *Policy Analysis.* In addition, Cato publishes the quarterly magazine *Regulation*, the bimonthly *Cato Policy Report*, and numerous books.

Center for Alternative Sentencing and Employment Services (CASES)
346 Broadway, 3rd Fl., New York, NY 10013
(212) 732-0076 • fax: (212) 571-0292
Web site: www.cases.org/education/cases

CASES seeks to end what it views as the overuse of incarceration as a response to crime. It operates two alternative-sentencing programs in New York City: the Court Employment Project, which provides intensive supervision and services for felony offenders, and the Community Service Sentencing Project, which works with repeat misdemeanor offenders. The center advocates in court for such offenders' admission into its programs. CASES publishes various program brochures.

Critical Resistance
1904 Franklin St., Suite 504, Oakland, CA 94612
(510) 444-0484 • fax: (510) 444-2177
e-mail: crnational@criticalresistance.org • Web site: www.criticalresistance.org

Critical Resistance is an activist group opposed to caging and controlling people in prisons, maintaining that prison is not an effective response to poverty and crime. The group advocates the immediate release of all nonviolent offenders from the U.S. prison system. It publishes several reports offering alternatives to incarceration on its Web site, including *A Plan to Save the State of California a Billion Dollars*.

Enterprise Prison Institute (EPI)
6009 Selvyn Ave., Suite 100, Bethesda, MD 20817
(301) 320-9180
e-mail: info@theepi.com • Web site: www.theepi.com

EPI is a private group that advises U.S. companies on how to develop prison-based production facilities. By promoting the use of low-cost inmate labor, EPI hopes to keep more companies from moving their manufacturing operations overseas. It publishes numerous articles on the advantages of prison labor on its Web site.

Families Against Mandatory Minimums (FAMM)
1612 K St. NW, Suite 700, Washington, DC 20006
(202) 822-6700 • fax: (202) 822-6704
e-mail: famm@famm.org • Web site: www.famm.org

FAMM is an educational organization that works to repeal mandatory minimum sentences. It provides legislators, the public, and the media with information on and analyses of mandatory-sentencing laws. FAMM publishes the quarterly newsletter *FAMM-Gram*.

Heritage Foundation
214 Massachusetts Ave. NE, Washington, DC 20002-4999
(202) 546-4400 • fax: (202) 546-8328
e-mail: pubs@heritage.org • Web site: www.heritage.org

The Heritage Foundation is a conservative think tank that advocates free enterprise and limited government. Heritage researchers support tougher sentencing policies and the construction of more prisons. Its publications include the quarterly *Policy Review* and online resources such as *Policy Research & Analysis*.

John Howard Society

809 Blackburn Mews, Kingston, ON K7P 2N6 Canada
(613) 384-6272 • fax: (613) 384-1847
e-mail: national@johnhoward.ca • Web site: www.johnhoward.ca

The John Howard Society of Canada advocates reform in the criminal justice system and monitors governmental policy to ensure fair and compassionate treatment of prisoners. It views imprisonment as a last resort option. The organization provides education to the community, support services to at-risk youth, and rehabilitation programs to former inmates. Its publications include the booklet *Literacy and the Courts: Protecting the Right to Understand.*

Law Enforcement Alliance of America

7700 Leesburg Pike, Suite 421, Falls Church, VA 22043
(703) 847-2677 • fax: (703) 556-6485
e-mail: editor@leaa.org • Web site: www.leaa.org

Comprising more than sixty-five thousand members and supporters, the Law Enforcement Alliance of America is the nation's largest coalition of law enforcement professionals, victims of crime, and concerned citizens dedicated to making America safer. It publishes the quarterly journal the *Shield.*

National Center for Policy Analysis (NCPA)

601 Pennsylvania Ave. NW, Suite 900, Washington, DC 20004
(202) 628-6671 • fax: (202) 628-6474
e-mail: ncpa@ncpa.org • Web site: www.ncpa.org

NCPA is a public-policy research institute that advocates more stringent prison sentences, the repeal of parole, and financial restitution for crimes. Publications include the periodicals *NCPA Policy Backgrounder* and *Brief Analysis*, which regularly address the issue of prisons. NCPA also publishes numerous papers and studies, including *Privatizing Probation and Parole* and *Crime and Punishment in America.*

National Center on Institutions and Alternatives (NCIA)

7222 Ambassador Rd., Baltimore, MD 21244
(410) 265-1490 • fax: (410) 597-9656
Web site: www.ncianet.org

NCIA is a criminal justice foundation that supports community-based alternatives to prison, contending that they are more effective at providing the education, training, and personal skills required for the rehabilitation of nonviolent offenders. The center advocates doubling "good conduct" credit for the early release of nonviolent first-time offenders in the federal prison system to make room for violent offenders. NCIA publishes books, reports, and the periodic newsletters *Criminal Defense Update* and *Jail Suicide/Mental Health Update.*

National Crime Prevention Council (NCPC)

1000 Connecticut Ave. NW, 13th Fl., Washington, DC 20036
(202) 466-6272 • fax: (202) 296-1356
e-mail: webmaster@ncpc.org • Web site: www.ncpc.org

NCPC provides training and technical assistance to groups and individuals interested in crime prevention. It advocates job training and recreation programs as a means to reduce crime and violence. The council, which sponsors the Take a Bite Out of Crime campaign, publishes the newsletter *Catalyst*, which comes out ten times a year.

Sentencing Project
514 Tenth St. NW, Suite 1000, Washington, DC 20004
(202) 628-0871 • fax: (202) 628-1091
e-mail: staff@sentencingproject.org • Web site: www.sentencingproject.org

The Sentencing Project seeks to provide public defenders and other public officials with information on establishing and improving alternative sentencing programs that provide convicted persons with positive and constructive options to incarceration. It promotes increased public understanding of the sentencing process and alternative sentencing programs. It publishes many reports on U.S. prisons including *Facts About Prison and Prisoners* and *Prison Privatization and the Use of Incarceration.*

Urban Institute (UI)
2100 M St. NW, Washington, DC 20037
(202) 833-7200
e-mail: paffairs@ui.urban.org • Web site: www.urban.org

UI is a nonpartisan research organization that conducts regular studies on a wide array of social issues. Its research on America's prison system maintains that inmates are not receiving enough rehabilitative programming or adequate life-skills preparation prior to release. Its reports on prison reform, posted on UI's Web site, include *A Portrait of Prisoner Reentry in Illinois* and *Parole in California, 1980–2000: Implications for Reform.*

U.S. Department of Justice
Federal Bureau of Prisons, 320 First St. NW, Suite 501, Washington, DC 20004
Web site: www.bop.gov

The Federal Bureau of Prisons works to protect society by confining offenders in the controlled environments of prisons and community-based facilities. It believes in providing work and other self-improvement opportunities within these facilities to assist offenders in becoming law-abiding citizens. The bureau publishes the book *The State of the Bureau.*

Vera Institute of Justice
233 Broadway, 12th Fl., New York, NY 10279
(212) 334-1300 • fax: (212) 941-9407
e-mail: info@vera.org • Web site: www.vera.org

The Vera Institute is an activist group that works to ensure a fair and efficient criminal justice system for all Americans. The institute takes the position that the country has incarcerated too many nonviolent offenders who would be better served by drug treatment and educational programming. It publishes the monthly *Issues in Brief* and numerous reports on prison reform such as *Diverting Drug Abusers from Prison* and *Project Greenlight: Preparing Prisoners for Release.*

Bibliography

Books

Andrew Coyle, Allison Campbell, and Rodney Neufeld, eds.	*Capitalist Punishment: Prison Privatization and Human Rights.* Atlanta: Clarity Press, 2003.
R.A. Duff	*Punishment, Communication, and Community.* New York: Oxford University Press, 2001.
Stephen Duguid	*Can Prisons Work? The Prisoner as Object and Subject in Modern Corrections.* Toronto: University of Toronto Press, 2000.
Joel Dyer	*The Perpetual Prisoner Machine: How America Profits from Crime.* Boulder, CO: Westview Press, 2000.
Joseph T. Hallinan	*Going Up the River: Travels in a Prison Nation.* New York: Random House, 2001.
Othello Harris, ed.	*Impacts of Incarceration on the African American Family.* New Brunswick, NJ: Transaction, 2003.
Tara Herivel and Paul Wright, eds.	*Prison Nation: The Warehousing of America's Poor.* New York: Routledge, 2003.
Joy James, ed.	*States of Confinement: Policing, Detention, and Prisons.* New York: Palgrave, 2000.
Robert Johnson	*Hard Time: Understanding and Reforming the Prison.* Belmont, CA: Wadsworth, 2001.
John Kleinig and Margaret Leland Smith, eds.	*Discretion, Community, and Correctional Ethics.* Lanham, MD: Rowman & Littlefield, 2001.
Ann Chih Lin	*Reform in the Making: The Implementation of Social Policy in Prison.* Princeton, NJ: Princeton University Press, 2002.
John P. May, ed.	*Building Violence: How America's Rush to Incarcerate Creates More Violence.* Thousand Oaks, CA: Sage, 2000.
Christian Parenti	*Lockdown America: Police and Prisons in the Age of Crisis.* New York: Verso Books, 2000.

Prisons

Joan Petersilia	*When Prisoners Come Home: Parole and Prisoner Reentry.* New York: Oxford University Press, 2003.
Alexander Tabarrok, ed.	*Changing the Guard: Private Prisons and the Control of Crime.* Oakland, CA: Independent Institute, 2003.
W. Gordon West and Ruth Morris	*The Case for Penal Abolition.* Toronto: Canadian Scholars' Press, 2000.

Periodicals

Vince Beiser	"A Necessary Evil? (Supermax Prisons)," *Los Angeles Times,* October 19, 2003.
Fox Butterfield	"Women Find a New Arena for Equality: Prison," *New York Times,* December 29, 2003.
Alan Elsner	"America's Prison Habit," *Washington Post,* January 24, 2004.
Julie Falk	"Fiscal Lockdown," *Dollars & Sense,* July/August 2003.
Nicholas Kulish	"Crime Pays: Since Census Counts Convicts, Some Towns Can't Get Enough," *Wall Street Journal,* August 9, 2001.
Eli Lehrer	"Hell Behind Bars: The Crime That Dare Not Speak Its Name," *National Review,* February 5, 2001.
Los Angeles Times	"Roads to Rehabilitation," November 25, 2003.
Ed Marciniak	"Standing Room Only: What to Do About Prison Overcrowding," *Commonweal,* January 25, 2002.
Ayelish McGarvey	"Reform Done Right," *American Prospect,* December 2003.
Edwin Meese and Eric Holder	"Work for the Chain Gang," *Washington Times,* July 23, 2002.
George Neumayr	"Crime and No Punishment," *American Spectator,* July 9, 2003.
Ernest Partridge	"The Two Faces of Justice," *Free Inquiry,* Summer 2001.
Amanda Ripley	"Outside the Gates," *Time,* January 21, 2002.
Kit R. Roane	"Maximum Security, Inc.," *U.S. News & World Report,* May 28, 2001.
Margaret Talbot	"Catch and Release," *Atlantic Monthly,* January/February 2003.
Sanho Tree	"The War at Home," *Sojourners,* May/June 2003.
Katherine Van Wormer	"Restoring Justice," *USA Today Magazine,* November 2001.
Richard D. Vogel	"Capitalism and Incarceration Revisited," *Monthly Review,* September 2003.
Edward Wong	"Behind Bars and on the Clock," *New York Times,* June 6, 2001.

186

Index

187